DEDICATION

Good first, always God first! He wrote the story of His plan for man through the ages. All I've done here is relay the message. The glory is His. I dedicate all to You.

Next, I dedicate this book to my son, Elijah. His childlike faith is both refreshing and inspiring. He is the next generation. I do not foresee Jesus tarrying for many more years, but if He does, may God help us and retain the unadulterated truth preserved in the pages of His Holy Word. America is quickly becoming a God forsaking country. Elijah, if you come to an older age and read your father's words, remember the faith instilled in you as a child and pray to God to increase it. You have always believed Jesus was coming back to get us. Your faith is unwavering. Keep that torch lit and share that light with everyone you meet. Jesus is coming soon, both for the saints and with the saints!

CONTENTS

7 RAPTURE VIEWS

PRE-TRIB

PAN-TRIB

MID-TRIB

PARTIAL

PRE-WRATH

PRETERISM

POST-TRIB

MILLIONS VANISHED

BRIAN PAUL LAKINS

www.MillionsVanished.com
For more information, please email: *1thes4.16@gmail.com*

Cover Design and Interior Layout *&* Design by
Quest Publications
Website: *www.questpub.questforgod.org*
Email: *questpublications@outlook.com*

Published By:
Quest Publications
6-176 Henry Street
Brantford, ON, N3S 5C8
Canada

ISBN-13: 978-0-9951872-4-5
ISBN-10: 099518724X

ABOUT THE COVER

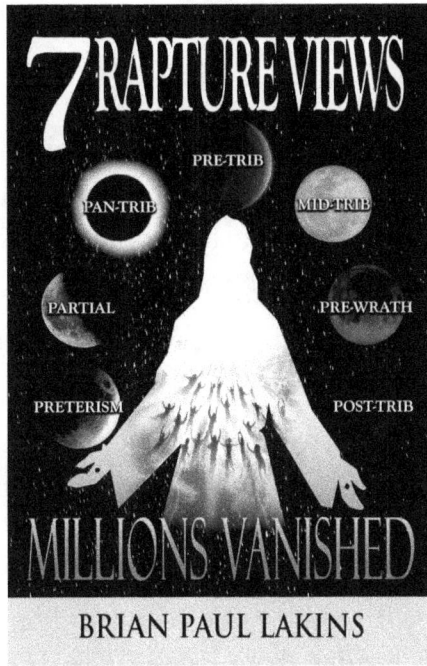

This will remain a mystery to those who breeze past the front matter of books. (Guilty)! To others, the cover was just an eye-catching hook that drew their attention away from the 100's of other books they glanced past. No matter what the case may be, the moon choices associated with each rapture view is not happenstance.

The evidence that flows from a watcher's keen researching skills is found and taught in book 3 of this series, The Watcher's Guide. The complete unveiling of the tid-bits I now give will have to wait until you begin your journey into book 3 (Visit this page again to bring more clarity after you finish reading this book).

I'm more excited about The Watcher's Guide than any other book in the Millions Vanished series! If you've had the rapture running through your red blood since the moment you first heard about it, then The Watcher's Guide is the information you dream about getting every time you watch a prophecy teaching broadcast.

1. Preterism—(partial lunar eclipse) This occurred 70 AD on Passover, the year many preterists believe the rapture happened, along with most prophecy, if not all.

2. Partial—(waning crescent) No significance with this moon selection. They hold to multiple raptures of church age Christians throughout the 7 Year Tribulation.

3. Pan-Tribulation—(total solar eclipse) No significance with this moon selection, just symbolism. This view has no definite timeline. They claim not to have enough light in Scripture to give a definite view. Thus, the moon selection of our physical light source being hidden, just as rapture knowledge is hidden from them by their own choice.

4. Pre-Tribulation—(first sliver of a new moon) This is always when the feast of trumpets begins.

5. Mid-Tribulation—(full moon) The mid-point of the Tribulation will be on Passover, which is always on a full moon.

6. Pre-Wrath—(total lunar eclipse / blood moon) This is when the pre-wrath view happens (Rev. 6:12). They believe this happens just before the end of the Tribulation, so I place it in that order, though Revelation 6 is actually toward the beginning of the Tribulation.

7. Post-Tribulation—The moon will be dark (Mat. 24:29), yet it will not be a new moon or a normal eclipse...

APPRECIATION

A special mention of appreciation must be given to Finis Jennings Dake. I am eternally grateful for his 43 years of dedication and passion of 100,000 hours of studying and teaching God's Word. I have received more in the past eight years from his Biblical knowledge and research through the Dake Annotated Reference Bible than I could have ever gotten from a lifetime of Bible college. His notes and references found throughout the 3,400 note columns with over 8,000 outlines are an invaluable resource that all of Solomon's riches could never replace.

INTRODUCTION

When is the rapture? Are you confused with which rapture timing view is correct? Do you believe a certain belief to be true, but cannot for the life of you validate why your belief is accurate, nor can you show someone from where in the Bible your view comes? Book 2 was written as an answer to book 1's silence on thoroughly addressing other views.

You don't have to know every single point and proof of every rapture view. There are pillars that can be proven that will shatter every other theory. The point of this book is to give a lifetime of security on this part of God's eternal plan, but without spending months or years learning it. This book gives the meat and potatoes of the rapture timing debate, and leaves out all the filler. This isn't to downplay or minimize the vast amount of research and writings from our church fathers and teachers of God throughout this age. It's just not the purpose of this book.

This unique book picks up where book 1 left off. Book 1, Unveiling Raptures and Resurrections, focused on teaching simple truths the Bible says about the subject of raptures, resurrections, and related topics, while defending the pre-trib view had mostly been laid aside. This book directly addresses rapture myths, perceptions, and truths, without side-stepping what is sure to offend or be divisive to those with an opposing perspective. My goal is to always present biblical truths in simple language, without belittling others in the process, but without wavering from teaching straight Scripture. Offense is never the motive, only harmonizing Scripture for sound doctrine.

If you read book 1 of the Millions Vanished series, then you already know that most rapture timing beliefs are correct since there is a pre-tribulation rapture, a mid-tribulation rapture, and two raptures at the end of the Tribulation, though the raptures at the end of the Tribulation occur at least 4 days before the Second Coming (More on that in books 3 and 4). There's been many types of raptures and many still to come, but the debates and arguments persist on one specific rapture, the rapture of the church.

This eye-opening and intelligently laid out book is geared to drive prophecy students straight to the heart of the debate without an excess amount of information in addressing every area from all views. Your time has been the consideration factor. For a subject on the rapture taking on every known view, this book was intentionally configured to give you a five-star dinner at a fast food pace. You will fully understand each and every view, why they believe what they believe, and where 6 out of 7 views have veered off course according to the harmony of Scripture throughout the Bible.

Reiterating what I said in book 1, a good education at a Bible college is a great way to be ahead of the game, but a good understanding doesn't have to take years. With this book, you will fulfill instantaneous results with Scriptural clarity and understanding that can only be compared to what steroids do for athletes. No matter what your reason is for picking up this book, you are taking the right course of action right now.

CHAPTER 1

PRETERISM RAPTURE VIEW

While I won't be giving a complete history of this view with its many differing points as conveyed from one preterist to another, I will give enough information to get a general picture. Preterism is the doctrinal term for the eschatological belief that the "end times" prophecies of the Bible have already been fulfilled. So, when we read what the Bible says about the tribulation, we are reading history. A preterist is a person who believes in Preterism, which is divided into two camps: full (or consistent) preterism and partial preterism. Full preterism takes an extreme view that *all* prophecy in the Bible has been fulfilled in one way or another. Partial preterists take a more conservative approach, and many partial preterists consider full preterists to be guilty of heresy.

There are many ideas within preterism, but we won't be taking on all these ideas. We will stick to their beliefs toward raptures and resurrections. Historically, preterists and non-preterists have generally agreed that the Jesuit Luis de Alcasar (1554–1613) wrote the first systematic preterist exposition of prophecy - *Vestigatio arcani sensus in Apocalypsi* (published in 1614) - during the Counter-Reformation, (also the Catholic Revival or Catholic Reformation) was the period of Catholic resurgence beginning with the Council of Trent (1545–1563) and ending at the close of the Thirty Years' War (1648), and was initiated in response to the Protestant Reformation. One of the earliest references that formed a basis for later preterism comes from Eusebius of Caesarea (c. AD 263–339).

The absolute earliest example of preterism may be found from the New Testament of the Bible. Hymenaeus and Philetus made shipwreck of their faith, erred from the truth, taught the resurrection was past, overthrew the faith of others, and were delivered to Satan by Paul (1 Tim. 1:19-20; 2 Tim. 2:17-18). Nothing more is known about these men than that, but one damnable error made was that they believed and taught that the resurrection was past. Full preterists believe and teach the same. The argument made by that camp of preterism is that this was written before the resurrection in or around 68 A.D., which is when they believe the resurrection happened. If that were true, then they would not be in error. However, we know the truth that Revelation was written at least twenty-five years after the destruction of Jerusalem in 70 A.D.

Preterism has been gaining ground by mostly converting pre-tribbers, those who believe the Rapture is before the Tribulation. I joined a Facebook group in 2015 that was for preterist. I wanted to learn more about what they believed and why they believed it so I could accurately learn where they were off and hopefully be able to persuade some. This may appear to be the wrong way to be unbiased and open-minded about a contrary view, but you'll soon learn why this was my stance. I learned a lot about preterism and preterists. They had a lot of disagreement within themselves, but this is no surprise, as even pre-tribbers disagree about many things.

For this reason, I have been motivated to write the foundational truths of all raptures and resurrections. A rather large surprise came my way when I continued to commune with preterists of all kind. I kept having preterist after preterist tell me they used to be pre-tribbers. This can only be because end-time teaching is seldom taught in churches, and when it is taught, it lacks a good foundation and substantial details are left out of the teachings. Some preterists have great depth to their beliefs and can teach it like no other. There are always those who can validate their beliefs, even when out of harmony with the entire counsel of scriptures.

Those who hold to partial preterism believe that the prophecies in Daniel, Matthew 24, Mark 13, Luke 21, and most of Revelation (with the exception of the last two or three chapters) have already been fulfilled and were fulfilled no later than the first century A.D. According to partial preterism, passages describing the tribulation and the Antichrist are actually referring to the destruction of Jerusalem in 70 A.D. and the Roman emperor Titus. There is no rapture to really speak of, though some partial preterists will say it is at the Second Coming when the righteous of the earth will join the armies of God in the sky. I guess they are okay with believing that they will have no preparation time in heaven for taking back the earth with force (Joel 2:1-11; Zech. 14:5; Jude 14-15; Rev. 19:11-16).

Full preterists believe the rapture happened sometime around 70 A.D., because some believe the Book of Revelation was written after Nero committed suicide in 68 A.D., and identify the Beast with another emperor. The Catholic Encyclopedia has noted that Revelation was "written during the latter part of the reign of the Roman Emperor Domitian, probably in A.D. 95 or 96." Many Protestant scholars agree. Full preterists only say this because it is detrimental to their claims if Revelation was written any time after 70 A.D., much less a quarter of a century later. There seems to be little proof of a year, as all years are not conclusive or credible for accuracy in authentic historical accounts. At the end of this segment on preterism, I'll bring the debate to a conclusion the old fashioned way, with context and proper interpretation.

Partial preterists do believe in the return of Christ to earth and a future resurrection and judgment, but they do not teach a millennial kingdom or that Israel as a nation has a place in God's future plan. According to partial preterists, the Bible's references to "the last days" are speaking of the last days of the Old Jewish Covenant, not the last days of the certain time periods. There are fourteen different end-time expressions, and none refer to the abolishing of the Mosaic Law, though it has been abolished, cast out, blotted out, taken away, and fulfilled (Mat. 5:17-18; Gal. 4:30; 2 Cor. 3:6-15; Eph. 2:15; Col. 2:14-17; Heb. 10:9).

The true meaning for "last days" is as follows: latter times - last years ending this age before the Millennium (1 Tim. 4:1), latter years - Armageddon and the end of this age (Ezek. 38:8, 16), latter days - the future tribulation (Num. 24:14; Dt. 4:30; 31:29; Jer. 23:20; 30:24; 48:47; 49:39; Dan. 2:28; 10:14), latter day - Millennium (Job 19:25), latter days - Millennium (Hos. 3:5), last days - end of this age preceding the Millennium (Dan. 8:19; 2 Tim. 3:1; Jas. 5:3; 2 Pet. 3:3; Jude 1:18), last day - the rapture, at least seven years before the Millennium and second advent (Jn. 6:39-40, 44, 54; 11:24), last days - the tribulation period or last seven years of this age (Acts 2:16-21), last days - first coming (Heb. 1:1-2), last times - first coming (1 Pet. 1:20), last time - apostolic times and the whole church age (1 Jn. 2:18), last time - second coming (1 Pet. 1:5), last days - Millennium (Gen. 49:1; Isa. 2:1; Mic. 4:1), and last day - end of the Millennium (Jn. 12:48; cp. with Rev. 20:7-15).

In order for preterists to maintain their position, they insist that the book of Revelation was written early (before A.D. 70). They must also use an inconsistent hermeneutic when interpreting prophetic passages. According to the preterist view of the end times, Revelation 6 – Revelation 18 are highly symbolic and do not describe any literal events. I'll pass on some rules of interpretation from the late Finis Jennings Dake. "It must be settled once and forever that the Bible does not contradict itself and all scriptures on a subject must be harmonized. It has a way of confusing its enemies and blessing its friends. The only thing difficult about the Bible is that it is a very large book and it will take time to master its contents enough to get a general understanding of it."

Let me be very blunt about the error of preterism that makes it even more dangerous than merely not understanding end-times. The full preterists claim that Jesus Christ returned in fulfillment of His promise to come back to take us to Heaven. They say Jesus returned in the person of the Roman armies to destroy Jerusalem and to excommunicate Israel, and Israel has been finished since 70 A.D. Now if that is not wicked, and if that is not twisting the scriptures, then I don't know what is. Jesus comes back to rescue Israel and regather them as a nation forever. I mean, you don't have to be a theologian or a scholar. This is just simple stuff from the Bible (Isa. 11:11-12; 14:1-2; 27:12-13; 43:5-7; 60:9-22; 66:7-8, 20; Jer. 3:17-18; 16:14-16; 23:3-8; 24:5-7; 30:3 – 31:40; 32:37-44; 33:7-26; 46:27-28; 50:19-20; Zech. 12:10-12; Zech. 12:10-12; Ezek. 11:17-20; 16:60-63; 20:33-44; 28:25-26; 34:11-31; 36:6-38; Ezek. 37 – Ezek. 39; Dan. 12:1; Hos. 1:10-11; 3:4-5; Joel 3; Amos 9:9-15;

Obad. 1:17-21; Mic. 2:12-13; 4:1-8; 5:3-15; Zeph. 2:7 – Zeph. 3:20; 8:1-8; 10:6-12; 12:1 – 14:21; Mal. 3:2-5; 4:1-6; Mat. 24:31; Acts 15:13-18; Rom. 11:25-29; Rev. 12).

Their problem is that they are led to believe in Replacement Theology. This antisemitism is a natural conclusion when they believe Israel has been replaced by the church. It leaves them open to be destroyed by Jesus at His literal coming. As you'll remember from book 1, many are gathered by the angels at the Second Coming to be judged on the basis of their treatment toward Israel through the time of the Tribulation. This is the Judgment of Nations (Mat. 25:31-46). Any preterist who actually survives through that literal and future Seven Year Tribulation will be condemned as a goat if they have not repented of their hatred toward Israel. Now, this claim against preterist is denied by them, as I have read many times on forums. But this is the case. Preterism is more dangerous than merely not believing in the future rapture of the church.

Be just as intelligent and rightful with the Bible as with any other book. Study it, not to disprove it, but to master its sacred contents and conform to its teachings and you will find it to be in unity. Many have been taught preterism and have believed it by the teachings of preterists. They have failed to learn the one simple and true rule of interpretation of the Bible, though there are several other solid rules. If we will just learn to take the Bible just as literal as any other book when at all possible, then we will be ahead of most and not lose the truth by the lies that seek to destroy us (John 8:44; 10:10).

When a passage cannot be taken literal, find the literal truth conveyed by the symbolic, figurative, or allegorical language used. Never change the literal meaning of Scripture to a spiritual, mystical, symbolic, or figurative meaning unless it is done by

God Himself. Take everything in the Bible literally unless this could not possibly be the meaning. When the language is used in a figurative sense, get the literal truth conveyed by it. For instance, in Revelation 12, there is a woman clothed with the sun, standing on the moon, and wearing a crown on her head made of stars. This cannot be literal, but it is not meaningless. There is a literal truth conveyed in this symbolism. The literal meaning of that symbolism has everything to do with Israel in the future, not the church.

Preterists make the mistake of making events of Revelation happen over the course of many hundreds of years. Since the destruction of Jerusalem did not involve the entire destruction of sea life as related in Revelation 16:3, or agonizing darkness as foretold in Revelation 16:10, then these judgments are interpreted by the preterist as purely allegorical. However, according to some forms of preterism, Revelation 19 is to be understood literally with Jesus returning physically, but chapter 20 is again interpreted allegorically by preterists, even though the thousand years are mentioned six times in Revelation 20:2-7. After that, Revelation 21 – Revelation 22 are understood literally, at least in part by some preterist, in that there will truly be a new heaven and new earth.

Preterists take the dangerous step of spiritualizing all passages of Scripture that relate to the nation of Israel, and claim that these refer to the church, the "New Israel." From 2 Peter 3, they teach that the "old earth," which Scripture says will pass away, is the Old Covenant. The new heaven and new earth, they say, is the New Covenant, and the "elements," which Scripture says will burn with fervent heat when this happens, are the "elements of the law." They cannot cease from horrible doctrine because of their poor eschatology (study of prophecy). That is the failure of preterism, making allegorical interpretations for anything they want, leaving the interpretation of Revelation to the opinions of the interpreter.

There have been worse times in the history of the world since 70 A.D., even if Jesus meant for Matthew 24:15-21 to be applied to the Jews only, which He actually did (Isa. 66:7-8; Jer. 30:4-7; Dan. 7:21; 8:9-14, 24; 9:27; Rev. 12). This is why the term "Jacob's Trouble" is synonymous with "The Great Tribulation," which is the last half of the Seven Year Tribulation when Antichrist breaks covenant with the Jewish people and two-thirds of the Jewish people are destroyed (Zech. 13:8-9; Dan. 9:24-27).

The partial preterist viewpoint leads to a belief in amillennialism, or postmillennialism, and is associated with covenant theology. Of course, it rejects dispensationalism. But its main problem is its inconsistent hermeneutic and its allegorizing of many biblical prophecies that are better understood literally. While partial preterism is within the range of orthodoxy, it is not the majority view among Christians today.

Amillennialism (Greek: a- "no" + millennialism) is the view in Christian eschatology which states that Christ is PRESENTLY reigning through the Church, and that the 1000 years of Revelation 20:2-7 is a metaphorical reference to the present church age, which will climax in the Second Coming. It stands in contrast to pre-millennialism, which states that Christ will return PRIOR TO a literal 1000-year earthly reign, which is literally the truth. Post-millennialism states that the Second Coming of Christ will FOLLOW a 1000-year golden age ushered in by the church. Preterists are more apt to believe the Millennial Reign of Jesus ruling and restoring the earth is not to be taken literal. delete rest of sentence after I replace beginning with this sentence.

Revelation 4:1 begins after the church is spoken of for the last time in Revelation 1 – Revelation 3. Greek: meta (NT:3326) tauta (NT:5023), after these things. This Greek phrase is used at the beginning and at the end of Revelation 4:1. The meaning is as follows: "After these things concerning the churches of Rev. 2-3), I looked ... a door was opened in heaven: and the first voice ... said, Come up hither, and I will show thee things which must be after these things, that is, after the churches (Rev. 4:1).

This confirms and settles the question as to the time of the fulfillment of all the events of Revelation 4 – Revelation 22. They must be after these things, that is all things concerning the churches, or after the rapture of the church. The church is no longer on earth when the events of Revelation 4 – Revelation 22 take place. The church age is represented by the prophetic application (Rev. 1:3) of the seven churches (Rev. 2 – Rev. 3). Revelation 4:1 is when the rapture takes place in Revelation and is the place that ends the church age.

Christ said the things of Revelation 4 – Revelation 22 "must be hereafter," that is, after the churches, as proved above and also by Revelation 1:19, which is the key to understanding the three main divisions of Revelation. If this is true, then the church is raptured before these things of Revelation 4 – Revelation 22, and after the things of the churches of Revelation 2 – Revelation 3. If "the things which are," from Revelation 1:19, concern the church (Rev. 2 – Rev. 3), then the "things which must be after" "the things which are" must concern events after the churches. The church must be here during the time of the fulfillment of the things concerning the churches, and it must not be here during the fulfillment of the things after the churches. Then the church is raptured in Revelation 4:1 between "the things which are" (Rev. 2-3) and "the things which must be hereafter," that is, after the churches (Rev. 4 – Rev. 22).

It was told to me by a preterist that "the things hereafter" are after John's life (of course there's no authority for that), but this person also maintained that Revelation 4 – Revelation 18 happened by 70 A.D. However, all sources point to John's death being around 98-100 A.D., meaning "the things hereafter" John's life were fulfilled 30 years before he died! This is the definition of contradicting one's self. The time of the rapture, like that of the Second Coming, is not definitely known as to the day or the hour, but we do know that it will take place before the Tribulation, before the reign of Antichrist (2 Thes. 2:1-8), before the fulfillment of Matthew 24 - 25; Mark 13; Luke 21; Revelation 4 – Revelation 19, and before the fulfillment of many other prophecies.

CHAPTER 2

PARTIAL RAPTURE VIEW

A t its most basic level of interpretation, the partial rapture view holds to multiple raptures of the church throughout the Seven Year Tribulation based on the believer's faithfulness. Some of the scriptures they use are: Matthew 24:40-51; 25:13; Mark 13:33-37; Luke 20:34-36; 21:36; Philippians 3:10-12; 1 Thessalonians 5:6; 2 Timothy 4:8; Titus 2:13; Hebrews 9:24-27; Revelation 3:3; 12:1-6.

These scriptures are a collage of Second Coming verses (Mat. 24:40-51; 25:13), resurrection verses (Lk. 20:34-36; Phil. 3:10-12), mixed with verses on watchfulness for the Second Coming (Mk. 13:33-37; Rev. 3:3), watchfulness and faithfulness for the rapture (Lk. 21:34-36; Tit. 2:13; 2 Tim. 4:8), statements of conditions for the rapture of the church (1 Thes. 5:6; Tit. 2:11-13), the fact that you can lose salvation (1 Cor. 9:24-27 (couple with the following eleven verses showing Israel also had salvation experiences, yet were cut off -- 1 Cor. 10:1-11), and a rapture reference for Israel (the man-child, or 144,000) in the middle of the Tribulation that is specific only to them as we have seen from our study in book 1 on those who make up the third phase of the first resurrection (Rev. 12:1-6).

The partial rapture view has been embraced by a small fragment of evangelical Christians, but has not been recognized by any evangelical Protestant group. The interpretation of the partial rapture is a whimsical discovery of an aspect about the rapture that seems to have a wider meaning of interpretation than the hope of the Lord's return for the saints. What they have going for themselves is an acceptance of more than one rapture, but they fail in interpreting their key verses correctly and arbitrarily developed more than one rapture of the church. All saints dead or alive will have their resurrection and/or rapture before the Tribulation. There will not be one righteous soul remaining on earth after the last trump is blown (1 Thes. 4:16-17; 1 Cor. 15:51-54; Rev. 4:1), and no more people making up the church will be raptured during the Tribulation.

The critics of the partial rapture view who are pre-tribulationists will often say, "The basic area of disagreement is whether a Christian who has been saved by grace can be denied translation or resurrection at the same time as those to whom He is joined in the one body of Christ. It is commonly held by evangelical Christians that salvation is by grace rather than a reward for good works. The believer in Christ is justified by faith, and receives the many benefits of salvation quite apart from merit or worthiness on his part."

They say this because the majority of pre-tribbers believe in unconditional eternal security, that is to say that salvation can never be lost or forfeited. Of course, Jesus did tell all His followers to pray that they'd be accounted worthy "to escape those things that will occur during the Tribulation" (to be raptured) (Lk. 21:36). I have spent much time on pre-tribulation rapture forums that were all ran by people who believed "once saved, always saved."

They weeded out all the pre-tribbers who believed Scripture clearly warned and taught otherwise, so it appeared like the majority of Christians believed that "once a son, always a son." I was eventually banned from them all. By my continued dialogues with professing Christians through time, I can honestly say the dominant belief is that a belief alone in Jesus will save a person no matter how they end up living through life. For those with understanding (Rom. 8:1-13; 12:1-2; 2 Cor. 6:14 – 7:1; Gal. 5:16-25; Eph. 1:13-17; Col. 3:1-10; 1 Thes. 4:1-7; Titus 2:11-13).

The partial rapture believers are correct in believing in more than one rapture. However, they are wrong in believing one's time of escape during the Tribulation is determined upon their level of faithfulness. In other words, they believe the very faithful will be raptured at the beginning or before the Tribulation, while the worldly believer would have to suffer the Tribulation until finally ready to be raptured at some point during, or at the end of the Tribulation.

The typical pre-tribber is correct in believing the rapture of the church is a one time event that is not sectioned off; however, they often lack the full understanding that there will be a middle or post-tribulation rapture for Israel (Dan. 12:1; Rev. 7:1-8; 12:5; 14:1-5), and the saints of the Tribulation (Rev. 6:9-11 coupled with Rev. 19:1-2), followed by the two witnesses (Rev. 11:7-12). They are also wrong in understanding the many phases of salvation.

The whole council of God on the matter has been given in the Word. John 3:16 is the greatest verse in the Bible on salvation, but it is not the entire teaching on the subject of salvation. Man is initially saved from God's wrath on sin by belief and repentance. By this, all his past sins have been taken away and forgiven (1

Jn. 1:9; 3:1-10). This is called initial salvation, which assures you of eternal salvation if you die at that moment, but most live on physically after initial salvation. We must walk faithfully with God to remain pure (1 Jn. 1:5-7; 2:3-6, 15-17; 3:1-3). If we do sin, then we must repent to become pure from the guilt of sin and unrighteousness again (Ezek. 18:24-32; Jas. 1:13-15; 5:19-20; 1 Jn. 1:9). Yes, the gospel tells us to stop sinning (1 Jn. 2:1-2; Jn. 8:11; 1 Pt. 4:1; 2 Tim. 2:19).

Finis Jennings Dake says, "Salvation is a hope and not actually an unforfeitable possession until the next life (Rom. 8:20-25; 1 Thes. 5:8; 2 Thes. 2:16; 1 Pet. 1:5, 9, 13). Eternal life is also a hope now, even though we possess it (Tit. 1:2; 3:7; Heb. 3:6; 6:11, 18-19; 1 Pet. 1:3, 13). It will not actually be an unforfeitable and an eternal possession until the next life and at the end of a life of sowing to the Spirit (Dan. 12:2; Mat. 7:13-14; 18:8-9; 19:28-29; Mk. 10:29-30; Lk. 18:29-30; Jn. 5:28-29; Rom. 2:7; 6:21-23; Gal. 6:7-8; 1 Tim. 1:16; 4:8; 6:12, 19; 1 Pet. 5, 9, 13; 3:7; 1 Jn. 2:25; Jude 1:20-24)."

The same conditions for going to heaven at death are in fact the same conditions for being raptured at the beginning of the Tribulation. At that time, the entire church will be caught up and eternally changed immediately after the souls living in heaven are resurrected and caught back up to Christ in the air (1 Thess. 3:13; 4:13-18). I guess the argument of who is going will continue no matter how much proof is given. It's true that the entire church will be a part, but who is the church? Ephesians 5:27 says the glorious church is who Christ is coming for, and even tells us how this church is defined. The glorious church does not have spot, or wrinkle, or any such thing. It should be holy and without blemish.

I tell you a great and powerfully sad truth now. The churches will not be emptied by believers. The churches may be filled after the rapture, and it is true that there will be a great revival after the rapture (Acts 2:16-21), but it is also true that many current church members will make up that great revival. So it is for this reason that I want people to call me a follower, because calling me a believer lumps me into the same category as worldly Christians who are not separate from the world (2 Cor. 6:14 – 7:1; Jas. 4:4-8; 1 Jn. 2:15-17). Calling me a follower implies holding a belief, while proclaiming obedience to that belief with that one simple word.

Salvation is an all-encompassing word of the gospel that takes into account all the rescuing acts and procedures found in the gospel program. There are several Hebrew and Greek words in Scripture that proclaim the whole truth of salvation or some phase of it. There are at least sixty phases of salvation, which takes into account, but also far exceeds the new birth and son-ship (Mat. 6:8, 9; Jn. 1:12; 3:1-18; Gal. 4:5-6; Heb. 12:7; 1 Jn. 3:1-3; 5:1-5, 10-18). A few of the many words are as follows: regeneration, washing, propitiation, deliverance, forgiveness, righteousness, restitution, faith, mortification, etc.

Three examples of these phases are as follows: repentance, which is a change of mind, a new mind about God (Mat. 3:2; 4:17; Lk. 13:1-5; 24:47; Acts 2:38; 3:19; 10:43; 2 Cor. 7:9-10; 1 Jn. 1:9). Conversion, which is a change of direction, a new walk with God (Ps. 19:7; 51:13; Mat. 18:3; Lk. 22:32; Acts 3:19; Jas. 5:19). Grace, which is a change of favor, a new standing before God (Jn. 1:16-17; Rom. 5:1-2; Eph. 2:1-9; Tit. 2:11-14; 2 Pet. 3:18).

Now, the overall point I am presenting is that the rapture subject is important to salvation, as it is one of the phases of salvation. Too many are being used by the enemy by silencing the doctrine of the rapture. They shut others down by saying they should be focusing on the Great Commission, not a divisive subject weaved into end-times doctrine. The truth taught from book 1 is that the teaching of the rapture is a great motivation for constant holiness.

Two phases of the sixty phases of salvation are glorification and destination. Glorification is a change of realm, a new dominion with God (Acts 3:13; Rom. 8:17, 30; 1 Cor. 15:21-58; Phil. 3:21; Rev. 5:10; 20:1-7). This is when Christ appears in the air and catches up the glorious church so that they appear as He is (Eph. 5:27; 1 Jn. 3:2-3). Destination is a related phase, which is a change of dwelling, a new home with God (John 14:1-3; Heb. 11:10, 13-16; 13:14; Rev. 3:12; 21:1-22:5). This is where those in Christ will be taken when Jesus translates the glorious church to the air and takes us back through a portal to heaven (Rev. 4:1; couple with Rev. 19:11 for proof of portal). After glorification, unforfeitable eternal security will be the reality for those translated (1 Cor. 15:51-54).

Although salvation and all its respective time periods that deal with sin are received in the initial stages by faith alone when one sincerely repents and believes the gospel, the various stages proceed in operation in the follower of Christ from the time of salvation until he obtains and comes into the concluding phase of salvation for man at the rapture and resurrection (1 Pet. 1:5-9, 13; Rom. 13:11; Heb. 1:14; Phil. 3:20, 21; 1 Thes. 4:13-17; 5:23; 1 Cor. 15:51-58; 1 John 3:1-3).

The majority of those in the faith would be surprised to learn that salvation even includes the redemption of all creation and creative activity at the end of the thousand-year reign of Christ and His saints (Rom. 8:17-25; Heb. 1:10-12; 12:25-28;

2 Pet. 3:10-13; Rev. 21, 22; Isa. 66:22-24). There was clearly no one act of deliverance for creation after the fall (Gen. 3; Rom. 5:12-21) since restoring creation back to pre-fall standards is a work of Christ and the saints for the Millennium, before God the Father brings Himself and the New Jerusalem to earth (Rev. 21 – Rev. 22). In the same light, it is simple to see how salvation takes in every stage of recovery for man in the process of deliverance from its start to its completion.

For a conclusion, let's recap what the partial rapture view is since we spoke thoroughly regarding salvation. Out of the 20th and 21st centuries, the partial rapture view has risen from the pre-tribulation rapture camp. There has arisen a minute group of pretribulationists who argue that only those who are faithful in the church will be translated at the pre-tribber timeline, and the remaining will either be raptured sometime during the tribulation or at its end before the Second Coming.

As expressed by one of the partial rapture followers, "The saints will be raptured in groups during the tribulation as they are prepared to go." He goes on to say, "The basis of translation must be grace or reward. …We believe that frequent exhortations in the Scriptures to watch, to be faithful, to be ready for Christ's coming, to live Spirit-filled lives, all suggest that translation is a reward." Their belief includes the concept that only the faithful saints will be resurrected at the first resurrection. This shows their misunderstanding of the phases of salvation in the first resurrection, as well as ignorance in what constitutes a saint. A saint is faithful, while a sinning saint is classified with the spiritually dead and sinners (Rom. 6:14-23; 8:1-12; Rev. 21:1-8; 22:14-15).

CHAPTER 3

PAN-TRIBULATION RAPTURE VIEW

Someone who professes to be a pan-tribber is either lazy in studying end-times, or a person who just doesn't want to offend or lose a following by their rapture timing view. Some people don't profess to be a pan-tribber because they just aren't current in the new theological doctrinal terms. I met a man at work who I asked about his rapture beliefs. This Catholic man said he just believes everyone who follows the Bible will be with the Lord in heaven one day. I commend him on his profession that it takes obedience to the Word to be raptured, but he really had no understanding of God's plan for man regarding these subjects. He was a pan-tribber without even knowing the terminology.

I know of two very well-known Christians who have Jewish roots. Individually, they each had amazing discoveries of the blood moons and the recent patterns of the Shemitah and Shavout, a period of seven years taught to Israel in the Old Testament. They both have actual rapture timing views as I found out when digging and researching them, but they both professed to be pan-tribbers. I can only assume they did not want to be divisive and lose their new following. We can't be like that, because being a "pan-tribber" was alien to Paul's teachings. He had a very short time with the Thessalonians, a little less than a month (Acts 17:2), and the first things he taught were the last things of this church age.

So many teach that the rapture is not an important enough doctrine to study and teach. Even while researching these other beliefs thoroughly for the sake of this book, I have read highly intelligent men proclaiming that the Bible really never says one view is better than the next. They have said we really can't know. The focus is always on the doctrines of the Virgin Birth, the Vicarious Atonement, the Trinity, Salvation by Faith Alone, and the Deity of Christ. Many pastors contend that the rapture is certainly not something that a new believer should give too much time or attention to, so for the sake of not going over anyone's head, most seldom even mention it, much less teach it.

The Thessalonians were Gentile and new converts who once served idol gods. They turned from these to serve the living and true God, and to wait for His Son from heaven (1 Thes. 1:9-10). How can one have the blessed hope of the rapture and wait for the Son of God to return from heaven if these truths are not taught (Tit. 2:11-13)? The point in all of this is that although the Thessalonians were new believers, Paul never hid the doctrine of the rapture from them. On the contrary, along with many other doctrines, he openly disclosed these teachings to them (1 Thes. 1:10; 2:12, 19; 3:13; 4:13-18; 5:1-11, 23; 2 Thes. 1:7-10; 2:1-12).

Who is someone to say "I'm a pan-tribber. It'll all work out in the end?" John MacArthur says, "Shame, O, for shame! when you ask them about the last things and how the story ends, they don't have a clue. They say, "Well I don't know if I'm a-mill, post-mill, pre-mill, pan-mill, whatever mill. I don't...but I don't think it's really important." That's like saying, you know, that a book is written, the most important book that's ever been written in the history of the world, the only book that truly reflects God's purpose for humanity and you don't care how it ends? Of course you care how it ends."

CHAPTER 4

PRE-TRIBULATION RAPTURE VIEW

I maintain the sound doctrinal correctness in the rapture of the church taking place BEFORE the Seven Year Tribulation is the dead-on view. There's already been a very solid presentation for the pre-tribulation rapture given using Revelation 1:19 as the key to accurately dividing the sections of the Book of Revelation, and giving Revelation 4:1 as the place in which the rapture of the church takes place. For the sake of being thorough, evidence is being given for the most common views, while explaining biblically why they are not correct by showing what the evidence is truly saying. This is not to bring anyone down for opposing the pre-tribulation view. I'm only seeking to bring a correct understanding so eagerness and hope will be dominant in the believer's lives. We can all be ready.

There's an in depth and thorough book to be written to establish without a shadow of a doubt that the rapture of the church takes place before the Tribulation, but this is not that book. There's also just as much to be written to prove or disprove the other timing beliefs of the rapture of the church, and again, this is not that book. I'm only pointing out some of the main reasons used for all these views in order to validate the claims throughout this book for the timing of the rapture of the church.

To start out this section, I want to give a quick argument for the rapture of the church and Old Testament saints being before the Tribulation starts. In the beginning of Luke 21:34-36, Jesus spoke directly to His disciples in regard to all genuine Christians who would be found worthy to "escape all these things" to be able to "stand before the son of man." Pay attention to the underlined words.

> And take heed to yourselves, lest at any time your hearts be overcharged with surfeiting, and drunkenness, and cares of this life, and *so* that day come upon you unawares. For as a snare shall it come on all them that dwell on the face of the whole earth. Watch ye therefore, and pray always, that ye may be accounted worthy to escape all these things that shall come to pass, and to stand before the Son of man (Lk. 21:34-36).

Take heed to "yourselves," or you that are living on earth after the rapture and during the tribulation (Lk. 21:8-11, 25-36; Mat. 24:15-22; Rev. 6 – Rev. 19). Context proves the events of the Seven Year Tribulation are what believers are to pray always for in order to stay mindful and holy, free from the condemnation of sin, so that they can stand before Jesus at His coming. In Luke 21:7, the disciples asked when the destruction of Jerusalem would take place, as just predicted (Lk. 21:6). They also asked what sign will there be when these things shall come to pass? Luke 21:12-24 was fulfilled in the destruction of Jerusalem in 70 A.D. Luke 21:8-11, 25-36 are unfulfilled and will only be fulfilled by the events happening in the Tribulation.

If you're following along in your Bible, notice that verses 8-11 are in fact about the Tribulation time by proof of the beginning of verse 12, which starts off, "But before all these." This refers to the destruction of Jerusalem in 70 A.D., while Luke 21:8-11 happen after that, which we know will be fulfilled in signs of the Second Coming of Christ by way of all the things listed in Luke 21:1-11, 25-33; Matthew 24:1 – Matthew 25:46; Mark 13, and Revelation 4:1 – Revelation 18:24. So Jesus had answered when the destruction of Jerusalem would be in verses 12-24, and then He answered the second question in verse 7 by continuing giving signs of His Second Coming (Luke 21:25-36).

There really is no other way believers (who are literally followers as clear language suggests) could be found worthy to escape those things except to be raptured before these events take place. Death is never a biblical means of escape, but always means to not suffer or have to endure punishment. In this case, the punishment is referred to as "these things," but are listed as ten signs in verses 8-11. What else could Scripture mean by standing before the Son of man? If the rapture were to take place at the Second Coming, then no man would be able to escape the peril found on the face of the earth.

But Scripture does makes evident that the wrath of God begins at the sixth seal of Revelation 6:12-17, in the first 3½ years of the Tribulation, and this wrath from Himself is in no way appointed for the church. His wrath is for the ungodly world (1 Thes. 5:1-11). Paul said, "God hath not appointed us to wrath, but to obtain salvation (deliverance) by our Lord Jesus Christ," so that both the dead and the living in Christ can live together in the rapture (1 Thes. 5:9-11). In view of this deliverance, we are to be comforted by the mystery revealed (1 Thes. 4:18) of the catching up of all those in Christ (1 Thes. 2:19; 3:13; 4:13-18).

Those in Christ will therefore rise "to meet Him in the air" and be received by Christ to go up to heaven to live with Him where His Father and the New Jerusalem are, which is where our mansions are (Jn. 14:1-3). After telling "us," the ones alive and in Christ (1 Thes. 4:16-17) that we will not be appointed for God's wrath (1 Thes. 5:9), Paul finishes his letter to the Thessalonians with one last rapture reference.

> And the very God of peace sanctify you wholly; and *I pray God* your whole spirit and soul and body be preserved blameless unto the coming of our Lord Jesus Christ (1 Thes. 5:23).

If you want to look in your Bible, you'll see that 1 Thessalonians 5:17 says to "pray without ceasing" in view of the rapture, while looking back a couple pages in this book, you'll see that Jesus said the same thing in view of the rapture, "pray always" (Lk. 21:36). They are both speaking of the same escape. The escape from the judgment of God's wrath, and also escape from the reign of the Antichrist as proven in the next chapters.

CHAPTER 5

MID-TRIBULATION RAPTURE VIEW

Mid-tribulationism teaches that the rapture occurs at the midpoint of the Tribulation. At that time, the seventh trumpet sounds (Rev. 11:15), the church will meet Christ in the air, and then the vial, or bowl, judgments are poured out upon the earth (Rev. 15 – Rev. 16) in a time known as the Great Tribulation. In other words, this view follows a line of logic that leaves the church in the seal and trumpet judgments, but gets raptured out during the last angel's trumpet blast, which they correspond to the last trumpet sound from 1 Corinthians 15:52.

This view has something going for it that the pre-wrath rapture believers don't have, as you'll discover in the next chapter. The mid-tribbers rightly divide the twenty-one judgments of Revelation in their correct timeline. They place the seven seals and the seven trumpets in the first half of the Tribulation, with the sounding of the seventh trumpet at the midpoint of the Tribulation. The pre-wrath rapture believers, like mid-tribulationism, believes that the church is caught up to heaven before the "great day of wrath" comes (Rev. 6:12-17), but the pre-wrathers believe the great day of wrath begins before the last seal is broken, and before the trumpet judgments.

In support of their view, mid-tribulationism points to the chronology given in 2 Thessalonians 2:1-3. They also rightly divide the events as follows: 1) apostasy, 2) the revelation of the Antichrist, and 3) the day of Christ (which begins at the Second Coming and is not the rapture as mid-tribbers assume). The mid-tribulation view teaches that the Antichrist will not be decisively revealed until "the abomination that causes desolation" happens (Mat. 24:15), which occurs at the midpoint of the tribulation (Dan. 9:27).

In other words, they do not believe this man of sin can be known until he breaks the seven-year treaty with Israel, enters the newly built temple, stops the Jewish sacrifices that will resume in that time, and declares himself God. They believe 2 Thessalonians 2:1-3 is saying the first 3 ½ years will begin the apostasy, then the Antichrist is revealed at the midpoint of the Tribulation, followed by the "day of Christ," or the Day of the Lord, which begins at the Second Coming through to the end of the Millennial Reign.

This doesn't make any sense in the arena of logic, faith, or simple understandings of facts and how they relate to the order of events. Logically, if the mid-tribulationists can understand who the Antichrist is when he breaks the infamous seven-year covenant with Israel, then they can most assuredly understand who the man is that signs this seven year covenant with Israel, especially with this seven year peace treaty being signed before the notorious events of the seven seals being broken and the seven trumpets being blown (Rev. 6, Rev. 8 – Rev. 11:15).

The truth is the revealing of the Antichrist is made known by his role in the Israeli peace treaty (Dan. 9:27). 2 Thessalonians 2:1-12 says two events must precede the Second Coming, which is the apostasy (2 Thes. 2:3; Rev. 9:20-21; 16:2, 9-11) and the revealing of the Antichrist (2 Thes. 2:3, 8; Rev. 6:2). 2 Thessalonians 2:1-12 goes on to say one event must happen before these two events, and that is the rapture of the church (2 Thes. 2:1, 7-8; Lk. 21:36; 1 Thes. 5:9; Rev. 4:1).

Mid-tribulationists use Daniel 7:2, which says the Antichrist will have power over the "saints" for three and a half years. To reinforce their view, they presume this is the first half of the tribulation and that the saints spoken of are the church saints. The simple truth is that saints, when spoken of in Scripture, are any company of redeemed men or women, and not specific to the church only. The saints before Israel (ex: Abel, Enoch, Noah, Abraham) were not the church (beginning during Jesus' ministry) and neither was Israel (ex: Joseph, Amram, Jochebed, Moses, Joshua, Samson, David). The Tribulation saints are just that, saints. The church is never once spoken of during the time of the Tribulation (Rev. 6 – Rev. 18).

Mid-tribulationalism also interpret "the day of Christ," found in 2 Thessalonians 2:2, as the rapture; therefore, the church will not be caught up to heaven until after the Antichrist is revealed. I hope you have a Bible open in order to look up these references to examine them for yourself (Acts 17:11; 2 Tim. 2:15), but in case you don't, we will need to see 2 Thessalonians 2:1-4 for ourselves for this next part.

> Now we beseech you, brethren, by the coming of our Lord Jesus Christ, and *by* our gathering together unto him, That ye be not soon shaken in mind, or be troubled, neither by spirit, nor by word, nor by letter as from us, as that the day of Christ is at hand. Let no man deceive you by any means: for *that day*

shall not come, <u>except there come</u> a falling away first, <u>and</u> that man of sin be revealed, the son of perdition; Who opposeth and exalteth himself above all that is called God, or that is worshipped; so that he as God sitteth in the temple of God, shewing himself that he is God (2 Thes. 2:1-4).

Now, if "the day of Christ" is the rapture (vs. 2), then it would be true that the Antichrist is revealed before the rapture, as well as the great falling away (apostasy) (vs. 3). To be clear, the rapture is only spoken of in verses 1 and 7, not verse 2, which is referencing the day of Christ. Verse one references both comings, the rapture for the saints in the air, and the Second Coming when Jesus comes with the saints to the earth. The rapture is referenced as "our gathering together unto Him." Verse seven references the rapture by saying, "until he be taken out of the way."

The day of Christ is often spoken of in reference to the rapture when Christ comes to receive saints unto Himself (1 Cor. 1:8; 5:5; 2 Cor. 1:14; Phil. 1:6, 10; 2:16). The Day of the Lord is the Second Coming through the thousand years until the end of the Millennial Reign (Joel 2:1, 11, 31; 3:13-15; Amos 5:18-20; Mal. 4:5-6; Acts 2:16-21; 2 Pt. 3:10-13; etc.). But here is the thing, the day of Christ is not always referencing the rapture, because by context, we can easily learn that sometimes it means the day of the Lord. 2 Thessalonians 2:2 is referring to the Second Coming, the first day of the day of the Lord.

This "day" is one of two times in Scripture when a day does not mean a twenty-four-hour time frame. Read 2 Peter 3:8-13 for proof, since it speaks of the renovation of the heavens and earth as part of the Day of the Lord, which happens at the end of the Millennial Reign. Verse 8 also reminds us and clues us in that a day is like a thousand years with the Lord, and visa-versa.

The day of God is another "day," and referenced in verse 12. It is when God rules supremely once again over all His creation without one person rebelling against Him, and as it was before Lucifer's and Adam's rebellions (Isa. 65:17; 66:22-24; 1 Cor. 15:24-28; Eph. 1:10; 2 Pet. 3:13; Rev. 21:1 – Rev. 22:5).

To prove that the day of Christ in 2 Thessalonians 2:2 is referring to the Second Coming, which begins the Day of the Lord, and is not the rapture, let's take it old school and look at some simple context. If the "Day of Christ" is in fact the Second Coming, then verses 3-4 are telling us that "that day shall not come, except" the falling away and the revealing of the Antichrist comes first. This truth is taught again in the same text. Verses 7-8 tell us the Antichrist cannot be revealed until the church (he) be taken out of the way (raptured).

> For the mystery of iniquity doth already work: only he who now letteth *will let*, until he be taken out of the way. And then shall that Wicked be revealed, whom the Lord shall consume with the spirit of his mouth, and shall destroy with the brightness of his coming (2 Thes. 2:7-8).

This double teaching along with the Revelation teaching (Rev. 1:19; 4:1) should be adequate in understanding the church is gone before the Antichrist is revealed. We will go very deep into this later.

Lastly, let's speak of the differences between the trump of God (1 Cor. 15:52; 1 Thes. 4:16-17; Rev. 4:1), and the angel trumpets being blown to initiate different stages of God's wrath. The mid-tribulationalists say the trumpet of 1 Corinthians 15:52 is the same trumpet mentioned in Revelation 11:15. They say the trumpet of Revelation 11:15 is the final trumpet in a series of trumpets; therefore, it makes sense that it would be "the last trumpet" of 1 Corinthians 15. The reference to a last trumpet must be understood in these last days so these errors in Scripture can be avoided and the truth be known.

As seen in the following passage, the last trump is not the last trumpet ever. This is a well-known Second Coming passage you've seen spelled out many times in this book already. It clearly shows a trumpet sound, even one from an angel. Even the mid-tribbers understand Matthew 24:29-31 to be a Second Coming reference, and they believe the rapture trumpet is blown by an angel.

> Immediately <u>after the tribulation of those days</u> shall the sun be darkened, and the moon shall not give her light, and the stars shall fall from heaven, and the powers of the heavens shall be shaken: <u>And then</u> shall appear the sign of the Son of man in heaven: and then shall all the tribes of the earth mourn, and <u>they shall see the Son of man coming in the clouds of heaven</u> with power and great glory. <u>And he shall send his angels with a great sound of a trumpet</u>, and they shall gather together his elect from the four winds, from one end of heaven to the other (Mat. 24:29-31).

> <u>Blow ye the trumpet</u> in Zion, and sound an alarm in my holy mountain: let all the inhabitants of the land tremble: <u>for the day of the LORD cometh</u>, for *it is* nigh at hand (Joel 2:1).

Joel 2 is another reference to a trumpet being blown at the end of the Tribulation. This trumpet is a call for war against the earth's rebels by the saints in heaven as context proves by Joel 2:1-11. Blowing the trumpet is a call to war (Joel 2:15; 3:1-16). Trumpets always sounded at gatherings of Israel (Ex. 19:13-19; Lev. 25:9; 1 Sam. 13:3; 2 Sam. 2:28), which is why the trumpet sounds in Matthew 24:29-31. The angels are gathering all Jews from around the world. This trumpet is predicted in Isaiah 18:3; 27:13; and Zechariah 9:14. These two trumpets at the end of the Tribulation are not the same as the seven trumpets of Revelation

8:2-6 in the middle of the Tribulation, or the trumpets in connection with the resurrection of the righteous (1 Thes. 4:16; 1 Cor. 15:51-58; Rev. 4:1), before the Tribulation.

So the question must be asked, "What does Scripture mean by the last trump? The answer has been hidden from the gentile church for centuries, especially during the dark ages when basic Bible knowledge was unknown because of the grasp of the religious leaders in those days. There really is a specific trumpet called the last trump, which is known by people who are educated in Judaism. This literal trumpet is blown once a year at sunset, ending the fifth feast of the Lord known as the feast of trumpets. There are seven feasts (Lev. 23), and they all have their fulfillment in the first and second advents of Jesus.

All the spring feasts were fulfilled at Christ's first coming, and on the exact day of the feast. All the fall feasts picture the second advent timeline, and the feast of trumpets is the first of the fall feasts, picturing the rapture. The feast of trumpets is when the "last trump" of the rapture of 1 Corinthians 15:52 is blown. Paul was telling the Jewish Christians when the rapture would be. In retrospect after seeing or knowing when the death, burial, resurrection, and outpouring of the Holy Spirit were, it would be blatantly obvious the feasts of the Lord that had been practiced and celebrated for over 1,500 years were simply dress rehearsals for the real thing. The feasts have been fulfilled in the order in which they have been given (Lev. 23).

The next feast, the fifth feast, is the next one in line to be fulfilled and matches the rapture perfectly. Coincidentally, the rapture is the next prophetic event to happen. The feast of trumpets is celebrated for two days, from sunset to sunset. We are told that the new moon and the feasts of the Lord are a shadow of things to come in Colossians 2:16-17. Since the Feast of Trumpets is the only Feast of the Lord that falls on a new moon, we should take particular note.

The Hebrew word translated "feast" also means "appointed time," so the seven feasts of the Lord are literally the seven appointed times of God. During the feast of trumpets, there are 99 trumpets blown during the two days, but the last trump is the 100th sound and is the one blown the very longest. It is believed that the last trump used in some rapture verses (1 Cor. 15:52; 1 Thes. 4:16; Rev. 4:1) is the same one specific to the last trump blown at the end of the feast of trumpets.

The truth is that the trump of God is a blessing that calls up the righteous and brings forth an event that will take place in a split second (1 Cor. 15:51-58; 1 Thes. 4:16-17; Rev. 4:1). The 7th trumpet judgment blast is to bring forth judgment and many events which are days in duration (Rev. 10:7; 11:15 – Rev. 13:18), and is one of the woes to men (Rev. 8:13; 11:15; 12:12). One is in front of the seven seals and first six trumpets of Revelation 6:1 – Revelation 9:21, the other is after these (Rev. 11:15). One is the trumpet of God, while the other is an angel's trumpet.

Interestingly enough, one of the events of the seventh trumpet is a mid-tribulation rapture, so with this knowledge from book 1 of the 144,000 being raptured at this point (Rev. 12:5), mid-tribulationism is correct as far as there being a rapture. The seventh trumpet covers a period of time (Rev. 10:7) and includes all the twelve great events of Revelation 11:15 – Revelation 13:18, so it can't be said with any kind of certainty that the 144,000 are raptured at the exact sound of the seventh trumpet (Rev. 11:15).

But in the days of the voice of the seventh angel, when he shall begin to sound, the mystery of God should be finished, as he hath declared to his servants the prophets (Rev. 10:7).

The mystery of God that should be finished refers to the casting out of Satan. It is to be finished during the days of the seventh trumpet (Rev. 10:7). The casting out of Satan has been predicted since Adam's day (Gen. 3:15; Isa. 24:21; 25:7; 27:1; Rev. 10:7; 12:7-12) and has been long delayed (Rev. 10:6-7). It is one of the 3 woes announced by the angel in Revelation 8:13 and Revelation 12:12. The casting out of Satan is necessary before the kingdoms of this world can become those of God the Father and God the Son (Jesus).

The entire sequence of events ushered in by the angel blowing the seventh trumpet is the announcement made (Rev. 11:15), the six statements of the elders (Rev. 11:16-18), the opening of the heavenly temple (Rev. 11:19), the travail of the sun-clothed woman (Rev. 12:1-2), the dragon's attack on the man-child (Rev. 12:3-4), the rapture of the man-child, or 144,000 (Rev. 12:5), the flight of the woman, or Israel (Rev. 12:6, 14), the war in heaven resulting in Satan being cast out (Rev. 12:7-12), the dragon's attack on the woman (Rev. 12:13-16), the dragon's attack on the remnant (Rev. 12:17), the rise of beast out of the sea (Rev. 13:1-10), and the rise of beast out of the earth (Rev. 13:11-18).

This announcement spoken of as one of the events (Rev. 11:15) is, "The kingdoms of this world are become the kingdoms of our Lord, and of his Christ; and he shall reign for ever and ever," but this won't be completed until the end of the Tribulation at the Second Coming (Rev. 19:11-21). The final banishment of Satan from heaven at his mid-tribulation war on God (Rev. 12:1-12) makes it possible for God to take over the governments of this world at the time of the Second Coming (Rev. 19:11-21).

The Millennial Reign after this is to set up His kingdom and is the last probationary period for man who enters into this kingdom by being a sheep or alive (Mat. 25:31-46; Dan. 12:12) at the time of the beginning of this thousand-year reign. After that, Christ will continue to reign forever and ever over the kingdoms of this world (2 Sam. 7; Isa. 9:6-7; Dan. 2:44-45; 7:13-14, 18, 27; Lk. 1:32-33; Rev. 11:15; 22:4-5). Saints shall also judge the world and rule forever under Jesus, the Messiah (Dan. 2:44-45; 7:13-14, 18, 27; Lk. 22:30; 1 Cor. 6:2-4; 2 Tim. 2:12; Rev. 2:27; 5:10; 12:5; 20:4-6; 22:4-5).

CHAPTER 6

PRE-WRATH RAPTURE VIEW

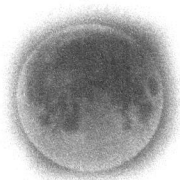

The pre-wrath rapture theory says that the rapture occurs before the "great day of wrath." Revelation 6:17 says, "For the great day of his wrath is come; and who shall be able to stand?" According to the pre-wrath view, believers go through most of the tribulation, but not the time of God's wrath just before the end of the tribulation. They use Matthew 24:21 as proof, which says, "For then shall be great tribulation, such as was not since the beginning of the world to this time, no, nor ever shall be."

What they are doing is assuming the "great day of wrath" from Revelation 6:17 is the same time frame as the great tribulation that Jesus was speaking of in Matthew 24:21, which is after the time the Antichrist breaks the seven year covenant he made with Israel, which is done half way through the Tribulation (Jer. 30:4-7; Dan. 9:27; 11:40-45; 12:1, 7, 11; Rev. 7:14; 11:1 – Rev. 19:21). This is easier proven by going back six verses from Matthew 24:21 to see that this is true.

> When ye therefore shall see the abomination of desolation, spoken of by Daniel the prophet, stand in the holy place, (whoso readeth, let him understand:) (Mat. 24:15).

This marks the starting point of the middle of Daniel's 70th week, the Seven Year Tribulation, when the Antichrist will break his 7-year covenant with Israel and enters Judea to take over Jerusalem as his capital and the Jewish temple as his capital building (Dan. 9:27; 11:40-45; 12:1, 7; 2 Thes. 2:4; Rev. 11:1-2; 12:1-17; 13:1-18). The entirety of this prophecy from Matthew 24:15 on must be fulfilled during the last three and a half years of this age.

Here is what confused me when I was studying this view. I know that Revelation 6 is at the beginning of the Tribulation, and I know the pre-wrath places the rapture and resurrection of the church and Old Testament saints at this time, yet they also claim the saints will endure most of the Tribulation. What finally made sense to me is the understanding that the pre-wrath rapture view makes most the Tribulation happen in Revelation 6, while the next ten chapters happen rather quickly, sometime in the last half of the Great Tribulation, or very near the Second Coming at the end of the Tribulation. They believe the last fourteen judgments, which are the seven trumpets and the seven vials, are contained in the seventh seal of Revelation 8:1.

Remember the chronological sequence of Revelation 1? Keep that in mind and you'll see that the glorious church will not see anything from earth's view after Revelation 4:1. What I really want to do is to show another way Scripture teaches the pre-tribulation rapture, which is perfect for showing the pre-wrath theory completely wrong. There are other aspects to the pre-wrath view, but all I'm going to do is to take on what I've made known so far and the other pre-wrath beliefs will simply collapse.

What pre-tribbers and pre-wrathers completely agree upon is that the Antichrist is revealed in Revelation 6:2, which says:

> And I saw, and behold a white horse: and he that sat on him had a bow; and a crown was given unto him: and he went forth conquering, and to conquer.

For those who believe differently, the white horse rider of Revelation 19:11-21 is not to be mistaken for this man riding on a white horse from Revelation 6:2. Jesus is undeniably and without refute from any view, the rider of the literal white horse from Revelation 19. This one in Revelation 6 is symbolic. The introduction of the Revelation 6:2 rider begins a series of dreadful events on earth, while the rider in Revelation 19:11-21 puts an end to these events.

The riders of the Apocalypse are symbolic because hell is the last rider, and hell is not really a spirit person, and neither is death, despite popular opinion (Rev. 6:8). War and famine are also not literal beings riding on horses (Rev. 6:4-6). War and famine are the results from the rise of the Antichrist (Rev. 6:2). Death and a great number going to hell at death is the result of war and famine.

The Antichrist comes on a white horse, imitating Christ and claiming to be Him (Rev. 6:2; Dan. 9:27; 11:37; Mat. 24:4-5; Jn. 5:43). He has a bow in his hand, which in symbolic language in dealings with men is always connected with evil designs and conquests (Ps. 7:12; 11:2; 37:14; 46:9; 58:7; Jer. 49:35). Jesus is never pictured as having a bow, but rather as having a sword (Rev. 1:16; 19:15, 21). I was always brought up with the teaching that the Antichrist will bring forth world-wide peace, which is why he is pictured as having a bow with no mention of arrows.

Yet, he is even said in the same verse as one who goes forth conquering and to conquer. He has been given great power by the god of this world (2 Cor. 4:4; Mat. 4:1-11). God's Word makes it clear that Satan is the one who gives Antichrist a crown (Dan. 8:24; 11:38-39; 2 Thes. 2:8-12; Rev. 13: 2-4), so we must understand this rider to be the Antichrist.

If the Antichrist is not being referred to here, in Revelation 6:2, then the 13th chapter is the first place in Revelation the Antichrist is mentioned. Why would he not be mentioned at the beginning when he rises to power? The truth is that he is the result of the first seal being broken and the next three seals are the result of this man coming to power to conquer as the Book of Daniel also foretells (Dan. 7:23-24; 8:23-25; 9:27; 11:36-45). This rider will cause the wars, famines, pestilences, death, and hell of the following 3 seals (Rev. 6:3-8). The personification of Hell is actually the fifth rider, though only four riders of the Apocalypse are ever referred to. Hell is the natural result of the wars, famines, and pestilences upon an ungodly people.

Without the passages in Daniel taught to us regarding this man of sin's area of conquest, also with the number of kingdoms conquered, the identity of the conqueror, his rise to power, and other facts could not be correctly understood. But putting these passages together with the facts from the revealing found from the Book of Revelation (Rev. 6:1-2; 13:1-18; 14:9-11; 16:13-16; 17:1-17; 19:19-20), we have the complete revelation of the Antichrist. If you don't accept the passages in Daniel and the passages in Revelation as being indistinguishable, then we can know nothing regarding the identity of the white horse rider from Revelation 6:2 and he would be a complete mystery.

I have read that the pre-wrathers believe the church will endure Satan's fury and man's persecution, but will be spared

God's wrath. What they are saying is that the church will be caught up to heaven before God pours out His final judgment on the world. The pre-wrath rapture view says the trumpet and the bowl judgments of Revelation 8 – Revelation 16 are the wrath of God that the church is exempted from (1 Thes. 5:9).

They are mostly correct in saying this. There are twenty-one judgments found by identifying the seven seals, the seven trumpets, and then the seven vials. The first five seals are the result from the wrath of man demonically influenced by Satan. The sixth seal is the wrath of the Lamb, while the seventh is not anything. It just says the breaking of the seventh seal results in silence in heaven for the space of half an hour. The reason for this is not given. The rest of the judgments are the result of the wrath of God. According to the pre-wrath rapture theory, the church will be present to experience the first six seals.

Let's get down and dirty to address two main points that just don't harmonize with the pre-wrath view. The first is the order of Revelation. Second is to prove the church is taken before the revealing of the Antichrist, so the church must be raptured before the agreed upon revealing of the rise of power of this man found in Revelation 6:2, which is undeniably before the supposed rapture found in Revelation 6:12-17. We will be teaching the rapture of the church before the revealing of the Antichrist without using the Book of Revelation, because this was already accomplished by proving the rapture of the church is in Revelation 4:1.

First, the seven seals are broken successively before the blowing of the trumpets (Rev. 6:2 – 8:1). The 7 trumpets are to be blown successively between the seals and vials (Rev. 8 – Rev. 10:7). The first trumpet will be blown after the seventh seal and the last will be blown in the middle of the Seven Year

Tribulation. The 7th trumpet covers a period of time (Rev. 10:7) and includes twelve great events of Revelation 11:15 – Revelation 13:18. The twelve great events are as follows: The announcement (Rev. 11:15), the 6 statements of the elders (Rev. 11:16-18), opening of the heavenly temple (Rev. 11:19), travail of sun-clothed woman (Rev. 12:1-2), the dragon's attack on man-child (Rev. 12:3-4), rapture of the man-child (Rev. 12:5), flight of the woman (Rev. 12:6, 14), war in heaven where Satan is cast out (Rev. 12:7-12), the dragon's attack on the woman (Rev. 12:13-16), the dragon's attack on the remnant (Rev. 12:17), rise of beast out of the sea (Rev. 13:1-10), and the rise of beast out of the earth (Rev. 13:11-18).

The 7th trumpet blows in the middle of Daniel's 70th week, for there is a period of 42 months (Rev. 11:2; 13:5), 1260 days (Rev. 11:3; 12:6), or 3½ years from this trumpet to the Second Coming (Rev. 12:14; Dan. 7:25; 9:27; 12:7). If the 7th trumpet sounds at this point, then the first 6 trumpets blow before this and the 7 seals are fulfilled before the trumpet. Therefore, the 7 seals and first 6 trumpets will be fulfilled in the first 3½ years of Daniel's 70th week (Rev. 6:1 – Rev. 9:21).

The seven vials are found in successive order after the last trumpet is blown (Rev. 15 – Rev. 16). These vial judgments happen in the last 3½ years of the week and are completed at the time of the Second Coming. Contrary to some teaching out there, the seven trumpets are not found in the seventh seal, and the seven plagues from the pouring of the seven vials are not found in the seventh trumpet. These twenty-one judgments are literally twenty-one separate events that take place in successive order, and easily proven by the references found above in Revelation.

As for the missing chapters from the references above, they are parenthetical references that sometimes contain whole chapters, like Revelation 7; 10; 14; 17 and 18. A parenthetical passage contains explanatory matter about that which will transpire in between two events. It brings more detail about the matter and may include the whole story of a matter taking place over a period of years, even though the parenthetical passage is all written out in one place, and without interruption of other events through those same years. To hammer this home, parenthetical passages are inserted between the main events, which explain certain things that are to happen along with the main events, but are not the same as these events.

For example, all of Revelation 7 is inserted in between the sixth (Rev. 6:12-17) and the seventh seals (Rev. 8:1), even though the events of Revelation 7 speak of the martyrdom of the Tribulation saints during the Great Tribulation (Rev. 7:14), or last 3½ years of the Tribulation. This is inserted in between the last seal judgments, even though the trumpet judgments have not been said to have happened yet, though all seven trumpets are blown before the Great Tribulation begins. The beginning of Revelation 7 introduces the 144,000 Jews who are awakened to the gospel truth at the beginning of the Seven Year Tribulation. A parenthetical passage is simply inserted in the right place in the story to explain other events. A simple understanding can be given by the use of an analogy. A story about a mass shooting might be told by verbalizing what you saw, but then giving a quick update on the condition of the victims before giving the rest of the details.

There are nine parenthetical passages in Revelation and they are found here: Revelation 7:1-17; Revelation 8:2-6; Revelation 8:13; Revelation 10:1 – 11:14; Revelation 14:1-20; Revelation 15:2-4; Revelation 16:13-16; Revelation 17:1 –

18:24; Revelation 19:1-10. This has been proof that the seven trumpets and the seven vials are not taking place at the very end of the Tribulation and the bulk of the Tribulation is not found in only eleven verses (Rev. 6:1-11) of the entire Book of Revelation that consists of twenty-two chapters (Rev. 1:1 – Rev. 22:21).

This sequential order of the Book of Revelation coupled with the knowledge that the rapture of the church takes place in Revelation 4:1 will help you stay clear of many false teachings, which far exceed believing in the pre-wrath rapture theory. Here is a fantastic example! A former pastor of mine taught a familiar belief that the Chernobyl event in Russia could have been the sounding of the third trumpet in Revelation 8.

If you are unfamiliar with this 1986 disaster, Wikipedia can help quickly catch you up to speed. "The Chernobyl disaster (also referred to as Chernobyl or the Chernobyl accident) was a catastrophic nuclear accident that occurred on 26 April 1986 at the Chernobyl Nuclear Power Plant in the town of Pripyat, in Ukraine (then officially the Ukrainian SSR), which was under the direct jurisdiction of the central authorities of the Soviet Union. An explosion and fire released large quantities of radioactive particles into the atmosphere, which spread over much of the western USSR and Europe.

The Chernobyl disaster was the worst nuclear power plant accident in history in terms of cost and casualties. It is one of only two classified as a level 7 event (the maximum classification) on the International Nuclear Event Scale, the other being the Fukushima Daiichi nuclear disaster in 2011. The battle to contain the contamination and avert a greater catastrophe ultimately involved over 500,000 workers and cost an estimated 18 billion rubles. During the accident itself, 31 people died, and long-term effects such as cancers are still being investigated." (End of Wikipedia).

Chernobyl means bitter. The asteroid thrown to earth in Revelation 8 is named Wormwood, which also means bitter. A smart and well known man named Irvin Baxter who has an end-time ministry by the same name, End-Time Ministries, also teaches the blowing of the third trumpet was fulfilled by Chernobyl. He also teaches the first and second trumpets were fulfilled by the first and second world wars. He has well researched the parallels and makes a compelling case.

The issue is that all of Revelation 4 – Revelation 22 are "after these things," (Rev. 1:19; Rev. 4:1) that is after the things concerning the church age (Rev. 2 – Rev. 3). All confusion and wrong understanding concerning end times could be better and simply understood if we would all comprehend that nothing after Revelation 4:1 can happen during the church age. Simply stated, the first few trumpets sound in Revelation 8, so this cannot take place until after the rapture of the church.

A correct understanding that Revelation is given in sequential order, with parenthetical passages inserted throughout to explain events or subjects further or completely, will also help in understanding that the 200 million demons unleashed from the abyss (Rev. 9) are not the same company of beings as found in Revelation 16, which are human troops assembled for the greatest and last battle of this age. China does not send 200 million people for the Battle of Armageddon, at least not as proven from Revelation 9 or any other scripture. You just aren't allowed to randomly jump around in Revelation. For another matter, the seven seals are broken before the seven trumpets are blown, so when were the seven seals broken, which begin with the revealing of the Antichrist (Rev. 6:2)? So when was this man of sin revealed?

The most dynamite proof for disproving the pre-wrath view is found in 2 Thessalonians 2:1-12. In 2 Thessalonians 2:1-12, we have straightforward and clear grounds that the rapture will occur before the revealing of the Antichrist. Now, this is so clear that there are no less than ten different beliefs on who the restrainer is that hinders lawlessness until he (the restrainer) is taken out of the way (2 Thes. 2:6-8). Now, if I can show you how these statements are true by using simple interpretations, then wouldn't you believe that the rapture of the church cannot possibly happen in Revelation 6:12-17, since the revealing of the Antichrist is clearly in Revelation 6:2?

Remember these facts, and then I'll show, without any theological gymnastics, that these statements are true, proving through another avenue that the pre-wrath rapture is wrong. The church and Old Testament saints will be raptured before the Day of the Lord (2 Thes. 2:2). The Day of the Lord is the time of the Second Coming through the end of the thousand-year reign (2 Pt. 3:10-13; Rev. 20:1-7). So I am saying the rapture happens before the Millennial Reign begins. The rapture is also said to be before the Second Coming, before the revealing of the Antichrist, and before the future seven-year Tribulation (2 Thes. 2:3-8).

Let's lay some easily known facts from the letters to the Thessalonians so we can better understand who the "he" is that hinders lawlessness and is taken out of the way before the revealing of the Antichrist. The purpose of the second letter to the Thessalonians was to calm believers and assure them that the day of Christ (vs.2), which is the same as the Day of the Lord, had not happened yet. He states that the apostasy (the falling away) and the Antichrist must happen first, before the Second Coming and the Day of the Lord. Paul furthers explains that one thing must happen even before those two events. The rapture will happen first (2 Thes. 2:3-8). Paul had to write a second time (2 Thessalonians) that he did not write any letter that claimed he changed any of his doctrines from the first letter (1 Thessalonians).

Some false teachers had forged a letter from Paul. He was assuring them that he had nothing to do with such a letter (2 Thes. 2:1-3). He reminded them that they already knew the truth from him (2 Thes. 2:5) and urged them to stand fast in the truth (2 Thes. 2:15-17). His entire teaching shows that apostasy and Antichrist precede the day of the Lord and the rapture of the church precedes Antichrist (2 Thes. 2:1-12).

What is it that the Thessalonians already knew (2 Thes. 2:5)? We can learn what they already knew from the first letter to the Thessalonians. We know as well that Paul had gone to them in person for the period of almost one month (Acts 17:2). As in all Paul's epistles, he encourages them to continue in holiness. But what was specific in his first letter? The coming of the Lord is a very prominent subject in every chapter (1 Thes. 1:10; 2:12, 19; 3:13; 4:13-18; 5:1-11, 23). The comings of the Lord refer to both comings as seen in 2 Thessalonians 2:1. The coming in the air for the saints (1 Thes. 3:13; 4:13-18), and the coming of the Lord to the earth with the saints. With the dominance of the rapture being taught to the Thessalonians, let's move forward to the understanding of who the "he" is that is taken out of the way before the Antichrist is revealed (2 Thes. 2:7-8).

There are no less than ten theories concerning the identity of the restrainer from 2 Thessalonians 2:7-8. They have been listed as follows: human government, Satan, the church, the

Holy Spirit, the power of God, gospel preaching, God's timing, the binding of Satan, the Jewish state, and last but certainly not least, Michael the archangel. Though I have read vast teachings on several of these beliefs, I want to make these as quickly taught as possible, only hitting a few theories.

Human governments will never be taken out of the world to permit the Revelation of the Antichrist. The Antichrist will be given the northern kingdom of the Old Grecian Empire at the beginning of the Tribulation. He will then make war with the other three kingdoms for three and a half years until he overtakes them in the middle of the Tribulation, when the other six kings hand over their authority to him and he revives the Old Roman Empire under one ruler, himself (Dan. 7, 8, 11; Rev. 13, 17). Before he controlled all ten territories, it was revised, not revived. The reason is the Old Roman Empire was under one ruler in ancient times, so even though the territory will be the same, until they are under the authority of one ruler, the empire will merely be revised, not revived.

After the Antichrist has control over all of the Old Roman Empire during the midpoint of the Tribulation, he breaks treaty with Israel and seeks to destroy her. God intervenes by sending the armies of the north to fight against the Antichrist's reign. He is busy fighting the northern forces for the majority of the Great Tribulation, when he finally conquers them and brings his entire forces to finish what he started three and a half years earlier at the midpoint of the Tribulation, which is to destroy Israel. And many other governments will be here in other parts of the earth throughout all the days that the Antichrist will be here (Zech. 14:1-5; Dan. 2:44-45; 7:9-14; Rev. 16:13-16). So the theory that the "he" of 2 Thessalonians 2:7-8 is human government has to be the wrong guess.

Another proposed answer is that Satan is the restrainer. It is believed that Satan has a carefully engineered plan to bring out his world ruler, but it must be at just the right time. For this reason, he is still holding back his secret weapon until the time when he will be most widely accepted. This is to believe that Satan has control over even the birth of the Antichrist, or to believe that Satan will enter into anyone he wishes. The truth is that only disembodied spirits, called demons, can enter into a person when one opens themselves up to such a possession. Satan does not know exactly when the Tribulation will be, so planning this man's birth is impossible, even if Satan did have the power to bring this man into being.

For example, Luke 22:3 speaks of Satan entering into Judas, but this must be understood with man being in union with Satan, being consecrated to the same end, one in mind, purpose, and life. There is no Scripture that teaches physical entrance of one being into another. Satan is an angelic being, and all angelic beings, like human beings, have a body. Understand that the Bible teaches man and woman becoming one, being in each other's plans, life, etc. So, Satan entering into Judas simply means Judas submitted to Satan's temptation to betray Jesus. He became one with Satan, like men become one in spirit with God when joined to Him in consecration (1 Cor. 6:17), yet man does not enter into God physically (Jn. 17).

Satan does not physically possess the Antichrist, and it is also clear that the Antichrist is a man, not the devil incarnate. Satan has not become man through a miraculous incarnation like Jesus did, nor can he through demonic conception. Other men through time will never be reincarnated to become the Antichrist. This is never taught in the Bible (Dan. 12:2; Jn. 5:28-29; 1 Cor. 15:20-58; Phil. 3:21; 1 Thes. 4:16; Heb. 9:27; Rev. 20:11-15). The Antichrist, the false prophet, and Satan are always presented as three separate beings (Rev. 13:2; 16:13-16). The Antichrist and False Prophet have their destination, while Satan is given another place of dwelling for 1,000 years (Rev. 19:20; 20:1-3, 10).

The Holy Spirit will never be taken from the world, for Jesus promised that He would abide with us forever (Jn. 14:16), not until the church is taken out of the way, no, not that. In Zechariah 12:10 – Zechariah 13:1; Matthew 24:14; Acts 2:16-21; Revelation 7:14; 19:10; and other scriptures we have much proof that the Holy Spirit will still be here throughout the tribulation and the reign of Antichrist. Therefore, He could not be the hinderer of lawlessness that will be taken out of the way. No Scripture ever says the Spirit will be taken out of the world. The door of mercy will never be closed to Jews or Gentiles and people will continue to be saved during the Tribulation when the Antichrist has been revealed (Acts 2:17-21; Rev. 6:9-11; 7:1-17; 12:17; 15:2-4; 17:17).

David Jeremiah, a pre-tribulationist, teaches that the "he" of 2 Thessalonians 2:7 is the Holy Spirit, though he agrees that people will be saved during the Tribulation. He teaches that the Holy Spirit will come upon man as He did in the Old Testament, even though Jesus said the Spirit will dwell with man forever (Jn. 14:16). I admire David Jeremiah, so I am not bashing him, but his influence is so great that I will address faulty teaching. He also teaches the rapture is found in Revelation 4:1, so any sighting of the Holy Spirit in heaven after that would prove He is the he of 2 Thessalonians 2:7.

He uses Revelation 4:5 and 5:6 to solidify his teaching. The Holy Spirit is seen in chapters 4-5 of Revelation as 7 lamps of fire (4:5) and 7 horns and 7 eyes (5:6). There is only one Holy Spirit (Eph. 4:4-6), yet He is referred to as the seven Spirits of

God (Rev. 4:5; 5:6). This is symbolic, for Jesus is referred to as a Lamb with 7 horns and 7 eyes, which are the 7 Spirits of God (5:6). This denotes His fullness and power upon the Lamb and before the throne.

To prove this, the Holy Spirit, also referred to as the seven Spirits in Revelation 1:4, is said to be before the throne. Revelation 1 is referring to what John had seen when the revelation was given to him (Rev. 1:19). No matter when you believe the Book of Revelation was written, it is unanimously agreed upon that it was written after Jesus had sent the Holy Spirit to earth, and Revelation 1 is absolutely before the church is raptured. So what this does is to prove that the Holy Spirit was still on earth when Jesus gave Revelation 1:4, although the Holy Spirit is said to before the throne in heaven. Revelation 1:4 has to harmonize with Revelation 4:5 and 5:6, so He is either not on earth dwelling with man now either, before the rapture, or He really is being denoted in His fullness and power upon the Lamb and before the throne.

In view of the considerable amount of references in the first letter to the Thessalonians concerning the church being taken away before God's wrath is poured out upon the earth (1 Thes. 1:10; 2:12, 19-20; 3:13; 4:13-18; 5:1-11, 23), I'd think it would be rather clear who the "he" is referring too. The church will be taken out of the world by rapture (Lk. 21:34-36; Jn. 14:1-3; Eph. 5:27; Col. 3:4; Jas. 5:7-8; 1 Pet. 5:4; Rev. 5:8-10; 19:1-10). It is the only one of the above mentioned hinderers of lawlessness that is to be taken out of the world, so it must be the hinderer that was known by the Thessalonians (2 Thes. 2:5-6). The rapture is spoken of in 2 Thessalonians 2:1, so how could we mistake who the "he" is referring to in 2 Thessalonians 2:7-8? The Thessalonians were never told in the first letter that the Holy Spirit would be taken out of the way.

Oppositions to this truth say, "The 'he' is not referring to the church because Revelation 13:7 specifically shows the Antichrist warring against the saints. Saints are definitely a part of the church." The truth is that all of God's people through the ages who have become redeemed are all saints, whether from the Old Testament, or New Testament. Those redeemed before the Law of Moses were called saints, just as much as Israel when in right standing with God, the church, and the tribulation saints. Just because one is a saint, does not ever automatically make them part of the church. People will be saved after the rapture, but not be part of the church (Rev. 6:8-11; 7:9-17; 13:7, 15-18; 15:2-4; 17:6; 20:4; Mat. 24:9-13, 22; Dan. 7:21-27; 8:24; 9:27; 12:7).

Another opposition to the "he" being the church is that people believe Jesus is coming back for His bride, which is feminine. The masculine word "he" could not be the wife of Christ for obvious reasons. People, pastors, and teachers are always saying Jesus is coming back for His spotless bride. They say it so much it is accepted as a Bible truth and fact, but no where in Scripture is that "truth" stated. The truth is that He is coming back for His spotless church (Eph. 5:27).

First, in no scripture is the church ever called the bride of Christ, though the fallacy can be found universally in commentaries, sermons, theological books, songs, forums, Facebook posts, and other Christian writings. Never once is this idea stated in the Bible itself, though Jesus does use what people understand to relate truths to them.

The Bible does reference the bride of Christ and tells us precisely who it is. The bride is the New Jerusalem in heaven that will be brought to earth at the end of the Millennium. An angel showed John and said, "I will shew thee the bride, the Lamb's wife" (Rev. 21:9-10). It was revealed to be "that great city, the holy Jerusalem, descending out of heaven from God." "And I John saw the holy city, new Jerusalem, coming down from God out of heaven, prepared as a bride adorned for her husband" (Rev. 21:2). The inhabitants of the Heavenly Jerusalem are called "his wife" in Revelation 19:1-10. The truth presented is that all the saved of all ages who will go to live in that city will become a part of the Holy City, which is the bride.

Some teachers say the church is referred to as a virgin. Paul was simply exhorting the Corinthians to be pure like a virgin, so like a father hopes to present his daughter to her husband as a virtuous virgin, so in like manner Paul wants to present his converts to God in all purity. The whole church is not cited here, only Paul's converts.

> Would to God ye could bear with me a little in *my* folly: and indeed bear with me. For I am jealous over you with godly jealousy: for I have espoused you to one husband, that I may present *you as* a chaste virgin to Christ (2 Cor. 11:1-2).

The truth of the matter is that Paul always used masculine pronouns when referring to the church. Paul wrote to the Ephesians and referred to the church as "the new man" and "a perfect man," which are masculine and speak plainly of the church.

> For he is our peace, who hath made both one, and hath broken down the middle wall of partition *between us*; Having abolished in his flesh the enmity, *even* the law of commandments *contained* in ordinances; for to make in himself of twain <u>one new man</u>, *so* making peace (Eph. 2:14-15).

Till we all come in the unity of the faith, and of the knowledge of the Son of God, <u>unto a perfect man</u>, unto the measure of the stature of the fulness of Christ (Eph. 4:13).

The body of Christ is the church (1 Cor. 12:13, 27; Eph. 1:22-23; Col. 1:18, 24). The Head of the body is Jesus, so why do we believe the body of Christ is feminine, while the Head of the feminine body is masculine? Therefore, the masculine pronoun in 2 Thessalonians 2:7 is correct in word study as well as context. Paul definitely said that the hinderer of lawlessness would continue to hinder lawlessness "until he (the church) be taken out of the way (raptured). And then shall that Wicked (Antichrist) be revealed," whom the Lord shall destroy at His second advent (2 Thes. 2:7-8).

With this proof established, we can see clearly that the Antichrist cannot possibly be revealed in Revelation 6:2, while the church is raptured in Revelation 6:12-17. The truth has been made known, and the rapture must happen before (2 Thes. 2:7; Rev. 4:1) the revealing of the Antichrist (2 Thes. 2:8; Rev. 6:2). The Antichrist is revealed in Revelation 6:2, but the rapture is in Revelation 4:1.

CHAPTER 7

POST-TRIBULATION RAPTURE VIEW

P ost-tribulationism teaches that the rapture takes place at the end of the Tribulation. The rapture happens at the Second Coming, immediately after the Tribulation (Mat. 24:29-31), almost simultaneously. At that time, the church will meet Christ in the air and then return to earth for the kickoff of the kingdom of heaven here on earth. According to this view, the church goes through the entire seven-year Tribulation and is caught up in the air right as Jesus and the heavenly saints and angels come through the portal for the battle of Armageddon (Rev. 19:11-16).

By this time, I believe the pre-tribulation rapture view has been well established, and I don't mean that as a self-appointed judge declaring my view as the winner. The best course of action for this chapter on the post-tribulation view is to take on their number one point of proof, the pillar of their belief, and touch on the rest. This will be very easy and brief, because these points have already been discussed in prior chapters. After that, the best path to take is to point out the many differences between the rapture and the Second Coming to see if they sound like they may be happening during the same event, or maybe happening as separate events.

The post-tribulationists best argument for their belief is Matthew 24:29-31. We've gone over and over this in detail, but I need to hammer it in your understanding. Please remain mindful of the underlined words.

> Immediately after the tribulation of those days shall the sun be darkened, and the moon shall not give her light, and the stars shall fall from heaven, and the powers of the heavens shall be shaken: And then shall appear the sign of the Son of man in heaven: and then shall all the tribes of the earth mourn, and they shall see the Son of man coming in the clouds of heaven with power and great glory. And he shall send his angels with a great sound of a trumpet, and they shall gather together his elect from the four winds, from one end of heaven to the other.

If you are not an avid reader of the Bible and you were taught the post-tribulation view from this passage, then it would be enough to convince. I have seen it many times. Matthew 24:29-31 is the number one passage given to me in times of debate. It is an amazing passage, and one that I hate to hear from the post-tribber, as with all scriptures used against sound doctrine. All scriptures on a subject must be present in order to harmonize them for a good doctrinal view.

Matthew 24:29-31 is undeniably about the Second Coming, which is agreed upon by all views. There is a two-fold reason this passage makes it look like the rapture is taking place at its fulfillment. First, the trumpet sounds, which is what happens at the rapture according to 1 Corinthians 15:52, 1 Thessalonians 4:16, and Revelation 4:1. Read these verses closely to follow the points ahead.

In a moment, in the twinkling of an eye, at <u>the last trump</u>: for <u>the trumpet shall sound</u>, and the dead shall be raised incorruptible, and we shall be changed" (1 Cor. 15:52).

"For the Lord himself shall descend from heaven with a shout, with the voice of the archangel, and <u>with the trump of God</u>: and the dead in Christ shall rise first: Then we which are alive *and* remain shall be caught up together with them in the clouds, to meet the Lord in the air: and so shall we ever be with the Lord" (1 Thess. 4:16-17).

"After this I looked, and, behold, a door *was* opened in heaven: and <u>the first voice which I heard *was* as it were of a trumpet talking with me</u>; which said, Come up hither, and I will shew thee things which must be hereafter (Rev. 4:1).

A theologian I highly respect and has taught me more about the Bible in six months than I had learned in the previous 29 years had said the last trump is when those alive and in Christ will be changed and raptured. By the name "last trump," he assumed there must be a first trump, which he claimed was the trumpet that sounded when those dead and in Christ will rise. He filled in the gap sort to speak, which makes sense since the dead rise first and the living go an atom of time after them.

By a careful reading of the "last trump" passage in 1 Corinthians 15, we see that only one trumpet is sounded for the dead to be raised "and we will be changed." That is, we which are alive, because "this corruptible must put on incorruption, and this mortal *must* put on immortality (15:53)." The word "and" is crucial. Two things happen at the last trump, not one thing for one trump followed by another thing for the last trump. There is no indication of more than one trump by the other two references either. The trump of God is what is blown for the dead and alive to be caught up (1 Thes. 4:16-17), and there is one voice like a trumpet bringing up the saints in Revelation 4:1, which is saying one thing with one voice, "come up hither."

As you learned in the mid-tribulation chapter, the last trump is what the special and specific trumpet is called that is blown at sunset to end the feast of trumpets in the fall, which is the next feast in line to be fulfilled (Lev. 23). Again, trumpets always sounded at gatherings of Israel (Ex. 19:13-19; Lev. 25:9; 1 Sam. 13:3; 2 Sam. 2:28), and this trumpet mentioned in Matthew 24:31 is predicted in Isaiah 18:3; 27:13; and Zechariah 9:14. This is not the same as the seven trumpets of Revelation 8:2-6, which are trumpets of angels blown during the first half of the Tribulation and do not sound past the mid-point of the Tribulation.

The Matthew 24:31 trumpet is also not the trumpet of God that sounds before the Tribulation starts, having no connection with the resurrection of the righteous (1 Thes. 4:16; 1 Cor. 15:51-58; Rev. 4:1). Also, proof of it not being the trumpet of God is the fact that an angel blows it. The angel in 1 Thessalonians 4:16-17 is using his voice, not a trumpet. We learn from Revelation 4:1 that the trump of God is from God, as that verse has a double meaning with the literal catching up of John in 95 or 96 A.D., and the foretelling of the rapture of the church and all Old Testament saints.

The second fact we learn from Matthew 24:31 that makes it look like the rapture is happening is that the elect are gathered together. As said earlier, though it may have gone unnoticed, is that trumpets always sounded at gatherings of Israel (Ex. 19:13-19; Lev. 25:9; 1 Sam. 13:3; 2 Sam. 2:28). The elect are being gathered by angels, which is never said in the previously reviewed references to the rapture and the sound of a trumpet (1 Cor. 15:52; 1 Thes. 4:16-17; Rev. 4:1). The reason is because the elect in Matthew 24 are speaking about the Jewish people, not the church.

We must not ever assume the church is always spoken of when the term "saints" or "elect" are mentioned. Any individual or group of individuals who have been chosen by God would be God's elect. There are many elects of God in Scripture, so determining who the elect is must be discovered by each passage where the word is found. For instance, even angels have been called the elect (1 Tim. 5:21). The entire chapter of Matthew 24 is Jewish in nature and context. The church has been raptured at least seven years prior from Matthew 24:29-31, and the elect here are the Jewish people who will be gathered at the Second Coming back to their homeland.

Post-tribulationists point out that the resurrection of the dead in Revelation 20:5 is called "the first resurrection." Post-tribulationists assert that, since this "first" resurrection takes place after the Tribulation, the resurrection associated with the Rapture in 1 Thessalonians 4:16 cannot occur until then. Let's read that verses and the following verse.

> But the rest of the dead lived not again until the thousand years were finished. This *is* the first resurrection. Blessed and holy *is* he that hath part in the first resurrection: on such the second death hath no power, but they shall be priests of God and of Christ, and shall reign with him a thousand years (Rev. 20:5-6).

This is the end of the first resurrection, which ends with the tribulation saints and the two witnesses (Rev. 6:9-11; 7:9-17; 11:12; 15:2-4; 20:4-6), completing the resurrection of all the righteous dead. The rest of the dead will be raised at the end of the thousand years, completing the resurrection of the unrighteous. The first resurrection clearly cannot be a one-day event, as Jesus began the first resurrection almost two thousand years ago, being the first fruit of the resurrection (1 Cor. 15: 20, 23).

All the resurrected saints are seen in heaven at the marriage supper of the Lamb (Rev. 19:1-10), which occurs at the end of the Tribulation, but immediately before the Second Coming (Rev. 19:11-16). Even the resurrected Tribulation saints are seen in heaven before the Second Coming.

> For true and righteous *are* his judgments: for he hath judged the great whore, which did corrupt the earth with her fornication, and hath avenged the blood of his servants at her hand (Rev. 19:2).

He avenged the blood of the saints at the hand of the great whore (Rev. 17 – Rev. 18), which is during the Tribulation. The following passage will be sufficient proof that the servants spoken of in heaven whose blood was avenged are the saints killed in the Tribulation.

> And when he had opened the fifth seal, I saw under the altar the souls of them that were slain for the word of God, and for the testimony which they held: And they cried with a loud voice, saying, How long, O Lord, holy and true, dost thou not judge and avenge our blood on them that dwell on the earth? And white robes were given unto every one of them; and it was said unto them, that they should rest yet for a little season, until their fellowservants also and their brethren, that should be killed as they *were*, should be fulfilled (Rev. 6:9-11).

Also, the fact that "much people" are in heaven here (Rev. 19:2) establishes they have been caught up in time for the marriage of the Lamb. This contradicts the belief of the post-tribbers who say no rapture of saints to heaven, only to the air to immediately return to earth. Revelation 19:2 also rejects the theory that the marriage supper of the Lamb will be held in the air after Christ raptures the saints (1 Thes. 4:16-17).

Post-tribulationists also rightfully point out that God's people have always experienced times of intense persecution and tribulation; therefore, the church will also experience all seven years of the Tribulation. In relation to this, the post-tribulational view differentiates Satan's wrath, or man's wrath, (Rev. 6:2-11) from God's wrath in the book of Revelation. Satan's wrath is directed against the saints, and God allows it as an implementation of purging His faithful. On the other hand, God's wrath is poured out on the Antichrist and his godless kingdom, and God will protect His people from that punishment.

The problem with God purifying "His faithful" is God gave His Son, Jesus, as payment enough. There is nothing man can do to purify himself, but after man is saved through faith alone with all past sins taken away, he is supposed to keep himself pure to stay pure (1 Jn. 3:1-10; 1 Tim. 5:20-22). Man is only to purify himself in the sense of keeping himself pure by refraining from sin by obedience to the gospel. Going through trials has never purified anyone, especially "His faithful," which would be an oxymoron. The faithful are already obedient, so purging is of no use for the faithful. The other problem is that there are multitudes of martyred saints in the Tribulation, so their claim of God keeping His faithful from harm is disputed in Scripture (Rev.6:8-11; 7:9-17; 13:7, 15-18; 15:2-4; 17:6; 20:4; Mat.24:9-13, 22; Dan.7:21-27; 8:24; 9:27; 12:7).

The best thing we can do now is to point out the many differences between the rapture and the Second Coming. When the rapture happens, all saints will "escape all these things that shall come to pass" during the Tribulation (Lk. 21:25-28), and will "stand before the Son of man" (Lk. 21:34-36; Jn. 14:1-3; 1 Thes. 4:16; 1-11; Rev. 5:8-10; 19:1-10), whereas at the Second Coming, all who are subject to punishment will not escape (Mat. 24:29-31; 25:31-46; 2 Thes. 1:7-10; Rev. 19:1-21).

At the rapture of the church, or the second rapture in the first resurrection, all saints will be presented to God in heaven (Eph. 5:27; 1 Thes. 3:13; 5:23), while at the Second Coming all raptured saints will be presented to the people on earth as their new rulers (Dan. 7:9-27; Rev. 2:27; 5:10; 20:4-6). The earth will finally be governed correctly. I know I can't be the only one who is tired of companies ruling like corporations, and corporations ruling like governments, always telling you soothing lies to subdue you while they rape you of your wages and ability to properly support yourself or your family. The Millennial Reign, or Dispensation of Divine Government, will set all straight in righteousness.

The godly minded person, or Christ-minded (1 Cor. 2:16), have the rapture as a goal to live with Christ in their mansion in heaven (Jn. 14:1-3; Col. 3:4; Jas. 5:7-8; 1 Thes. 2:19-20; 3:13; 4:13-18; 5:1-11, 23; Rev. 5:8-10; 19:1-10), while the goal in the Second Coming is to leave heaven for the earth to reign forever and set up the earth with righteous standards and impartial judges (Zech. 14; Jude 1:14-15; Rev. 11:15; 19:11 – Rev. 20:10). This is an amazing concept that lacks the full amount of detail. The glorified saints will be ruling on earth, yet have homes in heaven. Immortal saints will no doubt have the ability to travel at the speed of thought. The heavenly city of the New Jerusalem will be brought to earth at the end of the Millennial Reign. These mansions are where the city is and will always be. The location of the city is all that will change.

At the rapture, Jesus comes from heaven to the clouds only, not to the earth. His purpose is to take the good from among the bad (Jn. 5:28-29; 14:1-3; Lk. 21:34-36; 1 Cor. 15:23, 51-54; Phil. 3:21; Col. 3:4; 1 Thes. 4:16-18; Jas. 5:7-8), while at the Second Coming, seven years later (Dan. 9:27), He comes to the earth with His raptured saints to take the bad from among the good (Ezek. 38 – Ezek. 39; Zech. 14; Mat. 13:30, 39-43, 49-50; 24:29-31, 37-42; Jude 1:14-15; Rev. 19:11-21). Rest assured, all knees will bow before Jesus one day. You can't escape to the furthest galaxy, but why would you want to. His grace is sufficient to make you righteous if you just believe, repent from past sin, and obey His covenant.

During the rapture, Jesus comes from heaven to the clouds, not to the earth. His purpose is to receive the saints in Christ, the living and the dead, to take them to heaven (1 Thes. 4:16), while the Second Coming is a coming from heaven with the previously raptured saints to set up His kingdom and rule forevermore (Isa. 9:6-7; Dan. 2:44-45; 7:9-15, 18, 22, 27; Zech. 14:1-9; Mat. 25:31-46; Lk. 1:32-36; 2 Thes. 1:7-10; Jude 1:14-15; Rev. 11:15; 19:11-21; 22:4-5). Skeptics and rebels of the Bible always ask why God allows bad things to happen. Due to their dissatisfaction, the answer is that He will quickly put an end to all death, illness, and all around ungodliness.

At the rapture, there will be no great war, called the battle of Armageddon (Lk. 21:34-36; Jn. 14:1-3; 1 Cor. 15:23, 51-54; 1 Thes. 4:16), but the Second Coming of Christ with His saints and angels will intercept the Antichrist's army coming to destroy Israel and defeat him in the Valley of Megiddo, which is the battle of Armageddon (Ezek. 38 – Ezek. 39; Zech. 14; 2 Thes. 1:7-10; Jude 14-15; Rev. 16:13-16; 19:11-21). All warriors out there reading this, you will be a part of the greatest assembled battle in history if you are obedient to Christ. I am an aging warrior who finds joy in the hope of being this great of a fighter one day. Training for that day will be one of the many things the saints will be doing in heaven (Joel 2:1-11).

The rapture is an event that will take place during any given year and without any prophecy being fulfilled or any sign needed (1 Cor. 1:7; Phil. 1:7; 3:21; Tit. 2:13; 1 Thes. 1:10), while the Second Coming cannot take place until all of the predictions in Matthew 24 – Matthew 25; Mark 13; Luke 21:1-11, 25-33; 2 Thes. 2:7-8; and Revelation 19:10 have been fulfilled. The Second Coming will be easily predicted by the signing of the seven-year peace treaty with Israel (Dan. 9:27). In case that event is missed, the breaking of the covenant in the middle of the Tribulation will be sticking out like a sore thumb. This is when the Antichrist takes over the temple in Jerusalem, ceases the sacrifices, and declares himself to be God (Dan. 9:27; 11:40-45; 12:1, 7; Mat. 24:15; 2 Thes. 2:4; Rev. 11:1-2; 12:1-17; 13:1-18).

At the rapture, Jesus comes for the church, the hinderer of lawlessness, not to destroy the Antichrist or any other wicked man (2 Thes. 2:7-8). At the Second Coming, Jesus brings all the saints of all ages to destroy the Antichrist and millions of wicked men (Dan. 7:11; Joel 2:1-11; 2 Thes. 2:7-8; Jude 14-15; Rev. 19:11-21); see also (Ezek. 38 – Ezek. 39; Zech. 14; Mat. 24:37-42; 25:31-46).

When Jesus comes to catch up His saints at the rapture event, it will only be for those who are qualified. This means those who have all their past sins taken away and are living righteous lives, even if their time as being righteous has only been a few seconds (Ezek. 18:24-32; Lk. 21:34-36; 23:43; Jn. 14:1-3; 1 Cor. 15:23; 1 Thes. 4:16; Rev. 20:4-6). Only those who have repented from their sins to be born again will be changed from mortality to immortality and go to heaven (1 Cor. 15:51-54). At the Second Coming, all men qualified to live as citizens of the earth will be allowed to proceed as natural people into the next age, without any change from mortality to immortality (Zech. 8:23; 14:1-21; Isa. 2:2-4; 66:19-21; Dan. 2:44-45; 7:9-14; Mat. 25:31-46; 1 Cor. 15:24-28; Rev. 2:27-28; 11:15; 20:4-6), though they will live forever by eating of the tree of life as long as they remain conformed to God's ways (Rev. 21:27; 22:2, 14-15).

At the rapture event, no one will be sent to hell, but all saints will be taken to heaven (Lk. 21:34-36; Jn. 14:1-3; 1 Thes. 4:16; Rev. 5:8-10; 19:1-10). There will be a resurrection of all the righteous dead (1 Cor. 15:23, 51-54; Phil. 3:21; 1 Thes. 4:16), while at the Second Coming, millions of people will be sent to hell and none taken to heaven (Isa. 14:9-15; Mat. 13:30, 43-50; 25:31-46; Rev. 14:9-11; 19:20; 20:10). There will be no resurrection of any righteous people, because the first resurrection will then be over (Rev. 20:4-6).

The rapture is a going up in the air to meet Christ for those alive. Those dead in Christ, in heaven, will be coming back to the earth's atmosphere with Christ to be resurrected in their physical body to then be raised to meet Christ in the air. After that meeting in the sky, both companies of saved people of all past ages will go to heaven (Jn. 14:1-3; Col. 3:4; Jas. 5:7-8; Rev. 5:8-10; 19:1-10). During the Second Coming, both groups that were raptured will come back to earth through a portal in the sky (Rev.19:11). They will be accompanied by the 144,000, the Tribulation saints killed by the beast and the great whore, as well as the two witnesses (Zech. 14:1-9; Mat. 16:27; 24:29-31; 25:31-46; 2 Thes. 1:7-10; Jude 14-15; Rev. 19:11-21).

The last proof of a post-tribulation rapture that I'll speak on is found in Matthew 24:40. I've heard many pre-tribulationists teach on it when speaking of the rapture. The funny thing is that it is not a rapture of the righteous that Jesus is speaking of here.

> Then shall two be in the field; the one shall be taken, and the other left. Two *women shall be* grinding at the mill; the one shall be taken, and the other left. Watch therefore: for ye know not what hour your Lord doth come (Mat. 24:40-42).

This passage has always been taught to me as a rapture passage. The reference has been made by many prominent teachers in the end-time ministry field. There is a true view of the coming of Christ (vs. 37, 39, 42) suddenly when He is not expected for those that will be living on earth, and it's not the rapture of the church. The coming of Christ spoken of is the Second Coming, so be watchful (Mat. 24:37-42). The rapture is never once referred to in the entire book of Matthew. In the context all through Matthew 24 – 25, the unknown day and hour is always a reference to the Second Coming.

Taken like the flood "took them all away" (vs. 40-41) is a taking away for destruction, not to a place of safety like as in the purpose of a rapture. Luke 17:27 says the flood came and destroyed them all, that is to say the ones that needed to be destroyed, and saved Noah and his family. As we have learned throughout chapters 5-6, Jesus will destroy some at the Second Coming and leave some to replenish the earth in the Millennium (Zech. 14:16-21; Isa. 2:2-4; 66:19-21; Mat. 25:46; Rev. 20).

> They did eat, they drank, they married wives, they were given in marriage, until the day that Noe entered into the ark, and the flood came, and <u>destroyed them all</u> (Lk. 17:27).

The flood destroyed the people that it took away. They were taken by God's wrath, not taken to safety from His wrath.

There was no rapture in the event of Noah's flood. Likewise, the Second Coming will not rapture, or take any to safety, but destroy numerous amounts of people at the battle of Armageddon (Ezek. 39:17-22; Mat. 24:28; Lk. 17:34-37; Rev. 19:17-21).

CONCLUSION

God's plan for man is not to be ignored or taken lackadaisical. End-time subjects are too often brushed off as a non-issue and not important simply because the major portion of end-time doctrine is not salvational. The timing of the rapture may not matter to a person's eternal destination, but the correct understanding of these subjects is so important to God that He gave them all to man through many different authors, from slaves to kings, over many different centuries, on three different continents, written in three different languages, yet the converging facts from these different writers never contradict themselves.

As you have seen from this book, there are many subjects that delve off course because of the slightest sway of another subject. Ex: The "he" of 2 Thessalonians 2:7-8 leads many from believing the Holy Spirit will be here forever (Jn. 14:16). This even takes the plain focus away from the church being taken before the Antichrist is revealed. Believing many teachers who say the Book of Revelation is not given in sequential order has lead to mass confusion and a great multitude of diverse doctrine. The plan of God has been muddied up, yet it is given and simply understood for those who choose to harmonize all scriptures on the matter.

Another common deception is that end-time subjects are too confusing. Ironically, a large percentage of people who believe this also clump end-time teaching all into the Book of Revelation. Revelation actually means to reveal, or unveil, like when a new car is being completely shown when the cover is lifted off. The end-time subjects are spread throughout every major book in the Bible. The Book of Revelation brings clarity and harmony to these subjects, while even introducing new events and agents. As you've learned, confusion cannot be a crutch when an unveiling from God has occurred.

We can be led from ignorance. As many have proclaimed throughout my own life, "God is not the author of confusion." Christians have the Holy Spirit, so why the numerous amounts of teaching on the same subjects when we are using the same inspired, infallible, authoritative documents? Contrary to popular belief, the tempter who is the prince of darkness and current god of this world (2 Cor. 4:4) does not care if you and I believe the Bible is true and that Jesus is who He says He is. He knows he can't blind everyone from those truths, but he also knows his plans to deceive can still flourish like an inferno. You are now wiser and more aware.

Take Scripture at face value when at all possible, gathering together all verses on the subject, then harmonize them so all possible theories are dwindled away until there is only one that can stand. The one that stands is the one that is true. The part of the plan of God that concerns the rapture of the church has been set forth and now made clearly known to you. After very little study time, the rapture has become as easy to comprehend as John 3:16.

I'm so excited for the journey you've decided to go on. This is only the beginning folks! The greatest experience of your life is about to begin, and never end! All your life you've been told no one knows the day or the hour. You'll be awe-struck at how much you can actually know from Scripture, and how much God has intended you to understand from the beginning. The enemy wants us ignorant, not God! Make sure to get book three, *The Watcher's Guide*, and learn how close we are!

ABOUT THE AUTHOR

BRIAN LAKINS was ingrained into the Christian faith as a young child, but the temptations of the world to be a tough guy, worldly, and popular had lead him far away from God's path. Then, seeking his own ways for many years, the prodigal son returned to Jesus with an authentic passion and a God-given ability to write and speak to Christians and seekers, inspiring them to live holy in an unholy world.

He earned his Biblical Studies degree from Liberty University and is the founder of the Millions Vanished movement, which seeks to lead people away from entering the soon coming 7 Year Tribulation and lead the ones who do enter to eternal life by way of this book series, even after we have been taken to heaven. He believes what you leave behind can warn and save the ones left behind with clear biblical warnings and teachings to give the reader faith, hope, and power to live with valor and victory.

Brian has always been a grunt and a blue-collar worker who has continuously been surrounded by worldly unbelievers and believers alike. Wisdom has been gained in the trenches of life, and the passion for Brian to address deep questions of faith beyond surface teachings was produced. Keeping his hand on the pulse of the many modern Christian beliefs, Brian's analytical mind has developed him to be an expert in addressing relevant topics while anticipating and answering questions derived from all his teachings. Oddly enough, he never enjoyed reading or writing in his youth, but is now in-love with the researching process, excitedly treating it as if it were a treasure hunt.

FOR FURTHER CONTACT

Website and Contact:
www.MillionsVanished.com
1thes4.16@gmail.com
https://www.facebook.com/millionsvanished/
https://twitter.com/BrianLakins

OTHER BOOKS:

THE MILLIONS VANISHED SERIES
Unveiling Raptures and Resurrections (Part 1)
7 Rapture Views (Part 2)
The Watcher's Guide (Part 3)
Signs of His Coming (Part 4)
Billions Left Behind (Part 5)

THE OBEDIENT CHRISTIAN SERIES
My Road to the Path (Part 1)
Eternal Laws From God and Christian Warnings (Part 2)
Eternal Security's Evidence, Conditional Salvation's Verdict
(Part 3)
The Billions Who Lost Salvation From Genesis Through
Revelation (Part 4)
Tough Christian Questions, Tough Biblical Answers (Part 5)
The Lost Pillars of Conditional Salvation (Part 6)

www.ingramcontent.com/pod-product-compliance
Lightning Source LLC
Chambersburg PA
CBHW071456070426
42452CB00040B/1544